A MIRACLE FOR OUR TIME

A Miracle for Our Time

Studies in
Esoteric Christianity

Lona Truding

TEMPLE LODGE
London

Temple Lodge Publishing
51 Queen Caroline Street
London W6 9QL

First edition published by Temple Lodge 1990
Reprinted with minor corrections 1994

A catalogue record for this book is available from the British Library

ISBN 0 904693 22 8

Cover: art, Ivon Oates; design, S. Gulbekian
Typeset by DP Photosetting, Aylesbury, Bucks
Printed and bound in Great Britain by
Cromwell Press Limited, Broughton Gifford, Wiltshire

Contents

A Biographical Note on Lona Truding

Lona Truding was born in Vienna on 5 March 1901 and died in London on 26 April 1985. Her grandmother—who had many friends in the worlds of art and music, influenced the young Lona, who already had a great love and gift for music. She eventually decided—against the wishes of her father and with no financial support from her family—to study at the Conservatoire of Music. During these years she met many famous musicians, including Arnold Schoenberg. She also became a member of the Anthroposophical Society and began studying the works of Rudolf Steiner.

In 1939 Lona Truding came to England where she began to take an active part in the Anthroposophical Society and its activities. After the war she began to teach music in schools and universities. She also travelled frequently to the Goetheanum in Switzerland where she gave lectures on music, illustrated by demonstrations on the piano. These talks and performances are remembered with great fondness by those present. She also formed a deep friendship with Albert Steffen and many other personalities within the anthroposophical movement.

In 1966 Lona Truding underwent the amputation of her left leg. She overcame this disablement with enormous courage and was eventually able to lead a nearly normal life with the help of a small invalid car. It was at this point in her life that she began to lead a regular study group and gave lectures at Rudolf Steiner House in London. The lectures reproduced in this book demonstrate her wonderful grasp of Anthroposophy and insight into spiritual problems.

Editor's Introduction

Throughout this book the reader will notice many references and acknowledgements to Rudolf Steiner and the anthroposophical movement he established. Although Steiner was a philosopher—often frowned upon or completely ignored by the academic establishment for his radical and unconventional thinking—he is better known today for the practical initiatives which spring from his work. In the field of education, for example, a growing number of Steiner schools are to be found throughout the world. In farming the 'bio-dynamic' alternative agricultural methods are increasing in popularity. And in the medical world, as the old assumptions are being questioned, Steiner's ideas are becoming more influential. The reader may also have come across anthroposophical architecture, remarkable and often startling in its originality; or in the Arts the movement form known as Eurythmy. Steiner is also credited with impulses in painting, drama, economics, politics, healing education for the mentally and physically disabled—and the list goes on.

Behind this external work lies Anthroposophy (*Sophia*, wisdom); 'the knowledge of the nature of man'. Rudolf Steiner established the Anthroposophical Society with its centre at the Goetheanum, Switzerland, in 1923. From the years 1886 to 1924 he gave more than six thousand lectures and wrote twenty-eight books, many dealing with the above subjects, but all given from the perspective of the living reality of the spiritual world. Within this body of lectures are many dealing with deeply esoteric themes, most of which reveal wisdom that has been held back from mankind and preserved as 'mysteries' in various secret centres throughout the world. Steiner declared that, with the ending of *Kali Yuga* (the Dark Age), the time was ripe for the public announcement of such knowledge. His understanding of the Mysteries was, however, not based on external research but on a clairvoyant ability to read the Akashic Records.

Steiner warned against the reading of his lectures by those who did not already have some knowledge of his world-view, as given in his five most important books. For an exposition of this the reader is referred to *Occult Science, An Outline*, or *Theosophy*, both of which put forward ideas in the 'spiritual-scientific' manner which Steiner introduced to occult (i.e. that which is hidden from the physical eye) studies. *Knowledge of the Higher Worlds* is recommended for those seeking guidance in the Western path of initiation and the meditations required, while *Christianity as Mystical Fact* is a brief introduction to Steiner's teachings on Christianity. *The Philosophy of Freedom* is Steiner's major philosophical work, in which he argues for the scientific reality of the spirit. *

It is from Steiner's books and lectures, particularly those on Christianity and the concealed meaning behind the stories in the Bible, that Lona Truding draws much of the inspiration for her studies. Each chapter in this book is adapted from lecture notes for talks given by her at Rudolf Steiner House in London between the late 1970s and early '80s.

The lectures were open to the public but were usually given to audiences largely familiar with Anthroposophy. Hence the author sometimes takes for granted certain basic knowledge given in Rudolf Steiner's works. Amongst this knowledge is an elementary understanding of man's spiritual makeup; the history of the various planetary evolutions; reincarnation and karma; the meaning of Christ's incarnation on earth, and His mission for mankind. This may sound daunting to those not acquainted with Steiner's work, however the present volume has been compiled with the general reader in mind. *A Miracle for Our Time* will also be found to be an excellent introduction to esoteric Christianity and the teachings of Anthroposophy.

The subjects of these lectures may be seen to be varied, but the threads and themes which hold the work together are intricately woven. The central theme is Christianity—a deeper understanding of which many people are manifestly thirsting for at the present time. However it will be noted that an evangelical message, as understood in the traditional sense, is not evident here. The anthroposophical view of Christianity does not seek to convert or convince, but—respecting the freedom of the individual—is simply 'there' for those people seeking further knowledge of Christ.

Lona Truding takes us from Genesis and the Garden of Eden in chapter one, through to a final ending study of Steiner's *Philosophy of Freedom*, and the 'spirit-filled thinking' which it heralds. The journey between begins at the Mystery centre on the shores of the Black Sea, and an understanding of the missions of Zaratas, Scythianos and the Buddha (St Francis and Mani are also connected with the Black Sea Mysteries, as we see from their individual chapters). In her reflections on Christian Rosencreutz, Lona Truding argues that Rosicrucianism, and today Anthroposophy, bring together the two streams of Christianity and Buddhism. The chapter 'Manicheism Today' points us to a future stage of humanity's evolution when Mani's teachings will be truly fulfilled, while the chapter on the Three Kings explains that the gifts of the Three Wise

---

* All titles published by Rudolf Steiner Press, London.

Men represent more than the material substances of gold, frankincense and myrrh.

Modern materialistic thinking often leads us to bizarre conclusions about the Bible and Christianity, such as the common misconception of Christ's miracles as magic tricks or mere confirmations of faith. Perhaps such fallacies—including the current fad of rejecting anything in the Bible which sounds suspect to present-day scientific thinking; or the other extreme of taking every word in the Bible absolutely literally—are inevitable so long as a truly illumined spiritual approach is not undertaken. As Lona Truding explains in chapters five, six and seven, the miracles have deeply esoteric meanings. We see this in the latter chapter particularly, 'The Healing of the Man Born Blind', which centres on an act in the Gospels which is often misunderstood.

The book ends with the examination of four mighty, historical figures: Joan of Arc, St Paul, St Francis, and Raphael. It is revealed that they all further the goal of Christ in their own unique, mysterious ways. The individuality of Raphael is considered at great depth, and the fascinating development of his spirit in its various incarnations on the earth is revealed. And as we contemplate the individuality of Raphael, a vision arises before us of reincarnation as a positive evolution; not as a negative accumulation of 'bad karma', but a patient building and growing from experience.

Indeed, many Christians fear the doctrine of reincarnation because they view it as an excuse to 'opt-out' of the responsibilities of this life (a justified fear if the religious life degenerates). However, a profound Christian understanding of reincarnation and karma can only spur us on to a positive living of the present. The 'fire and brimstone' of an external Hell is no longer required to terrify us into choosing the Christian path. We need only reflect on the inevitable regret we will experience, during our life after death, over our current misdeeds and lost opportunities.

S.E.G.
December 1989

Additional Note: In preparing this edition (after the death of the author) the editors have sought to maintain the style and expression of Lona Truding. The reader should thus be aware that the contents of this book were originally given as lectures. Occasionally, quotations are paraphrased versions of original texts, although where possible references and other material have been checked against original sources.

1
The Garden:
Place of Temptation and Redemption

What actually is a garden? A garden is nature organised by man. First of all let us look at the Paradise Legend in simple folklore— in the Paradise plays of earlier centuries—as we know it in the *Oberufer Christmas Plays*. Here, in simple language, is a description of 'Paradise' or the Garden of Eden: [paraphrased version follows]

> 'How fresh the morning doth appear, before the sunrise we are here. In the beginning God did found the earth, and made the welkin round. He made the firmament also, and two great lights therein to show. The one is day, the other night, for God hath made them both aright. Yea beasts and plants both great and small, and at last by the great skill He made man and set in Paradise to dwell.
>
> And God gave man—Adam—the command over the whole creation the Garden of Eden. Take those the creatures of the field, Adam, to thee they are designed to do the Service in their kind. The whole creation I give to thy command. Share thou with me my domination ...'*

But man was not creative in the act or deed of creation. He could only share the fruits of what was given to him without his participation and therefore he lost what was never his.

To find out how the Paradise Legend fits into the whole evolution of mankind we have to hear and try to understand what Rudolf Steiner had to reveal to us from the Akashic Chronicles.[1] Rudolf Steiner says in his lectures on Genesis:

* *Christmas Plays from Oberufer* (London, Rudolf Steiner Press, 1973)

> 'When the Bible itself, after the "days" of creation, speaks of Paradise we must look for the deeper meaning behind this, and only spiritual science will enable us to understand the truth... It is only too clear in many accounts of creation—including the one in the Bible—that Paradise was not situated upon earthly soil, that it was lifted above the earth, was so to say in the heights of the clouds, and that while man lived in Paradise he remained a being of warmth and air. At that time man did not actually walk about the earth on two legs; that is materialistic fantasy... we have to think of man as a being belonging not to the ground, but to the periphery of the earth.'*

At that time of creation the nervous system was still embedded in the etheric body and appeared to the retrospective vision as a collection of wonderful plant-like beings, embedded in the ether body and the animal world threaded through it, so that we see Paradise, or the Garden of Eden, as a network of plant-like entities, extending in all directions. This collection of primitive plant-like entities, in which dwell the animal beings, as we have mentioned before, is seen clairvoyantly as the Garden of Eden. The condition of man was like that similar to sleep, when we look at the physical and etheric body from without, which we do every night. But it is that physical body which makes this sad impression on the seer because he recognises it as the last withered survival of a former splendour. And now the question arises: 'Who has made this form which I see clairvoyantly, this wonderful plant-being with the perfect animal-like structure in it; who has made it into the present shrivelled human body?' Then like an inner inspiration the answer rings out: 'You yourself by falling into temptation'. You yourself are responsible for what you are now. You had the power to integrate and impregnate all this splendour of the Paradise Garden with your own being. But man followed the persuasion of the snake, sowed the seed of death and all the former splendour shrivelled up, became arid, and was reduced to its present shrunken state. But Rudolf Steiner continues:

> 'The snake as an animal could never have persuaded man

* Rudolf Steiner, *Genesis* (London, Rudolf Steiner Press, 1982)

and tempted him to disobedience. At this moment there appears to him, worming his way amongst the primordial animal-beings of the Paradise Garden the wondrous form of Lucifer himself. For the first time we make the acquaintance with Lucifer who appeared within this cosmic order and such were his forces that the whole splendour of the Paradise Garden shrivelled up in the physical human body and this shrivelled state pressed man out of Paradise. He now lives in the world outside the structure which has shrunk and become the physical body. This contraction of the physical body brought about by Lucifer caused man to become heavier and sink down from the periphery to the surface of the earth through his own weight. So he had to leave behind him the Beings who form the clouds and the lightning—the Cherubim. Man falls to earth's periphery out of the regions where the Cherubim hold sway, and the Godhead placed a Cherub with the flame of the whirling sword before the Gates of Paradise.'

So Paradise is not to be found any more in a world which obviously no longer exists in the phenomenal world of today. Paradise, in the shrinking process of the physical body, had become a multiplicity of the inner organs of the physical body. The human being has been expelled and no longer lives in his inner being. Man had come to terms with the physical world and had to work on it by the sweat of his brow. Work had become a curse.

The Powerful Magic Garden

Lucifer has now taken hold of man's astral body. He who really experiences the Paradise Imagination as a reality, as a conquest of higher experiences, feels himself after the 'fall' gripped by an inner tumult of emotions—by an inner uncertainty of the soul. Man feels himself powerfully attracted by all passions and emotions which are the effect of our now living a personal life on the physical plane, and the forces of magnetic attraction—the personal interests we have gradually developed which work with ever increasing power. All these personal feelings and passions that we harbour in us are myriads of magnetic forces which also act as opiates.

This situation is precisely the layout of the Magic Garden created by Klingsor, a mighty luciferic being, a magnetic sorcerer whose aim it is to destroy through this Magic Garden the Knights of the Holy Grail. One can experience this at the opening of the second act of Richard Wagner's *Parsifal*, which I saw in my youth at the Vienna State Opera (the design and scenery were the same as suggested by Gustav Mahler).

Through magnetic forces Klingsor fetters the human soul to his command, even though this is against its will, so the character Kundry is caught up in Klingsor's tempting services. Her astral body, which was for many incarnations under the powerful influence of evil magnetism, is revealed in her former names ('Herodias was she and who else?', as emphasised in the opera). These forces of evil unfold in the Magic Garden as strange flowers, rootless. It is more a jungle than a garden. Everything grows in profusion and proliferates. The huge trumpet-like chalices trap insects; they are meat-consuming flowers living on the sap of other plants to which they cling. They are parasites, they give this garden a fearsome character and the flowers grow bigger, become more entangled, and he who enters the Magic Garden becomes a prisoner of his desires and passions. We might say that every desire leaves a hollow in the astral body. As soon as one desire is satisfied, the craving for another creates an even bigger hollow and so it continues until the victim is 'hooked', as we say today. The evil powers of the Magic Garden fetter and ensnare the human soul.

Now we see two different human beings attracted by the magnetism of the Magic Garden through Klingsor. With them we enter the domain of the Holy Grail which, as Rudolf Steiner shows, is intimately connected with the Paradise Legend. The Paradise Legend is given for the benefit of terrestrial humanity as it contemplates its origin. It is therefore given to enlarge man's horizon. The Grail Legend is given in order that it may penetrate into the inmost depths of the astral body, into its fundamental interests, which, if left to their own devices become egotistical and consider only personal interests. We must imagine Klingsor's Magic Garden in the realm of the astral plane and not on earth at all. Just like the Paradise Garden existed in the even higher sphere of *Devachan*.

Attracted to that sphere are mainly the Knights of the Holy Grail. Klingsor created it to destroy the whole knighthood out of hatred and envy (this is a historic reality proved by Wolfram von Eschenbach*) and they succumb to the temptation in their own different ways.

In this realm man can err in two different directions. Either he unites himself too deeply with the egotistical interests of his astral body, that also includes his environment, or not deep enough. The first category is that of Amfortas the King of the Holy Grail, the other is that of Parsifal who is only slightly interested in the affairs of his surroundings. The true development of man lies between the two as far as his astral body is concerned. His passions and desires, which he should have overcome, have infiltrated his self-hood which lives in his blood, and this is fatal. Amfortas is mortally wounded by the sacred spear (that once pierced the side of the crucified Redeemer so that all egotistical blood could flow out). Amfortas becomes a victim of the Magic Garden and now suffers more as his impurities cannot be healed.

But Parsifal the spotless soul also fails. Just as Amfortas was too much enmeshed in his desires so Parsifal is not sufficiently aware of what is happening around him. He is not sufficiently awake inwardly to ask in full self-consciousness the question: 'What is the meaning of the Holy Grail?' which he saw frequently carried into the hall, 'What does it demand?' It demands of King Amfortas to embrace the interests of all mankind and eradicate his own, after the example of the Christ.

In the case of Parsifal it is necessary that he should raise his interests above that of the mere innocent spectator of things, to the inner understanding of what is common to all men, of what is everyone's due—and in this case the gift of the Holy Grail.

The immense evolutionary value of the Grail Legend is that it could influence the soul of the Knights of the Holy Grail to balance these two attitudes of soul, and to raise the astral body to the ideal of universal humanity. Then the Magic Garden loses its significance, Parsifal regains the sacred spear from Klingsor and through it the garden withers and disintegrates and the words

* Wolfram von Eschenbach, *Parzival* (London, Penguin, 1987)

become truth: 'For where there are gathered together two or three in my name there I am in the midst of them', no matter where these two may be found in the course of terrestrial evolution.

The innocent Parsifal reunites the Holy Spear with the Grail Vessel, healing Amfortas' wound in the process of it.

For the transforming of the astral body from selfishness to a world-wide interest in all humanity, one important factor is necessary; the act of *renunciation*—to renounce the sheer personal interests with their desires, to give up these satisfactions, to refuse to find the easiest way out. We only develop through resistance. Renunciation is an act of man and the Gods alike, and this leads us into the Holy Land to the crossing of the Brook Kidron entering the Garden of Gethsemane.

The Garden of Gethsemane

This was a stage on which the greatest drama of mankind was performed to the words 'Not my will but Thy will be done!' The renouncing of all wishes of our personal will to the acceptance and enactment of the Divine Will. Let us recollect these words to be found in the Gospels: 'Am I not able to call forth a whole multitude of angels if I wish to avoid the death of sacrifice?'

This attitude is beautifully expressed in the painting of El Greco, *The Garden of Gethsemane*. In the centre, towering above the whole scene, the Angel bearing the Cup of Destiny. Kneeling before him Christ in red colour with dark insets but dissolving into yellow, the whole giving the impression of a flame. In the foreground the disciples seemingly fast asleep, although the beholder receives the impression that John is walking, moving in his sleep. In the background, in the pallid light of a half hidden moon, Judas with the Roman soldiers just entering the garden on Mount Olive. That which Christ might have accepted at that moment, to call forth the multitude of angels for his help, he rejected in resignation and renunciation. By having made it he himself allows the opponent Judas to enter his sphere. Christ renounced that which would have occurred if he had not allowed Judas to appear as his opponent. Judas enters the garden of agony and betrays Him to the Roman soldiers through a kiss. In order that the greatest immeasurable value might enter evolution Christ

Himself had to place His opponent in opposition to Him by the renunciation of the God Himself.

So the greatest mystery of all could happen on Golgotha and as the red blood flows from the Cross into the earth it glows up in the complementary colour, in radiant green. A total transformation takes place, that from man to man in the words from the Cross to the disciple: 'Behold thy mother'. That from man to nature, which is now redeemed through man and radiates a fresh new green. The proliferation of the flowers of the Magic Garden has turned into real growth in the innocent light of the first morning. This is, according to Richard Wagner, again the wondrous blessing of Good Friday. In a deeply moving description Richard Wagner speaks of this experience when, on the morning of Good Friday in 1857, he looked across the lake in Zurich and he saw the shimmering green of the growing, sprouting and blossoming nature, and he knew with clarity that this renewed verdant growth of nature was brought about through Christ's death on the Cross. He knew the connection with the secrets of the Holy Grail, and he realised that what through nature and man moves as desire is now chaste. The infinite innocence and chastity which slumbers in the chalice of the blossom had to transform the soul of man, now redeemed. This, Richard Wagner tells us in his *Parsifal*, is the reality of Good Friday.

Now we can enter the last Garden, the one of which the *Risen Christ is Master*, the Gardener. The purified human soul is chosen and awakened to recognise Him the very moment He calls her name: 'Maria'. But Maria—actually Maya or Miriam in Hebrew—is not a mere name but rather a virgin state of the soul.

We find a profound reference of this fact in Rudolf Steiner's *Fifth Gospel** and also in *The Gospel of St Luke*† how the mother of the Luke Jesus boy retained in her later age an original virginity as was the case before the birth of the Nathan Jesus boy.[2] So we have to recognise the state of the soul of Mary Magdalene who had achieved purity again and recognised the Risen Christ in her own

---

* Rudolf Steiner, *The Fifth Gospel* (London, Rudolf Steiner Press, 1985)
† Rudolf Steiner, *The Gospel of St Luke* (London, New York, Rudolf Steiner Press, Anthroposophic Press, 1988)

specific way, expressed by St John in the words 'she, supposing him to be the gardener' (St John 20:15). He *was* the Gardener.

The 'Garden of Resurrection' as I call it, is the vast realm of the Universal Cosmic Ether which individualized in the particular sheath of the Risen Christ where he is to be found today by all of us. In this etheric expanse both potentialities are living—that of Evil and that of Redemption.

As I started with the Paradise Legend so let me also finish with it. These words of Christ were spoken to the 'penitent thief' who was crucified with Him. To the request of the penitent thief: 'Lord remember me when Thou comest into Thy Kingdom', into this inner awareness of the malefactor of the meaning and significance of the 'Kingdom', likened in the parables to a seed, into this dawning recognition Christ could respond with a promise: 'Verily I say unto you, today shalt thou be with me in Paradise.'

2
The Mysteries of the Black Sea

At the north-eastern shore of the Black Sea, at the foot of the 7000 metre high, wild, craggy mountain range of the Caucasus—a bulwark against Russia—stood the ancient city of Colchis. We know Colchis from the Greek saga of the Argonauts and their quest for the Golden Fleece. It was the task of Jason to rescue a sacred lamb's Golden Fleece from the claws of a fierce dragon, who watched the Golden Fleece day and night, and return it to his people. With the help of the sorceress Queen Medea, who stupified the dragon, Jason was able to rescue the Golden Fleece for future evolution. The legend indicates the historical transition from the epoch of the Bull to that of the Ram or 'Lamb', i.e. the fourth post-Atlantean epoch, and with it the approach of the Christ Being to earth. Rudolf Steiner says that the Golden Fleece of the Lamb of God indicated the golden radiant astral body still undimmed by the approaching egotism of humanity. Thus the place Colchis was already imbued with the Sun-forces and already prepared to be the place for the sacred Mystery centre and school of the Black Sea.

We can ask what lies behind the foundation of the Mystery centre? In the early Christian era, about 400 AD, a great occult conference took place in the spiritual world, concerned with the initiation of Christian Rosenkreutz. He was associated with certain other great individualities who would lead the future civilisations of humanity. There were present not only personalities in incarnation on the physical plane but also those who lead a body-free existence in the spiritual world. Three individualities of the greatest significance for the evolution of humanity were the teachers of this Mystery school at Colchis: Zaratas (the reincarnated Zarathustra), Scythianos (the bearer of Manichean teaching), and the Buddha (who was not incarnated anymore but taught from his spirit body). These were the three great spiritual teachers whose thoughts streamed down from the divine spiritual world to impulsate those who visited this Mystery centre.

Zaratas, an incarnation of Zarathustra, could impart the wisdom of the Sun and Stars to his pupils. The greatest of them was Pythagoras who became aware of the music of the spheres as a disciple of Zaratas and through him of Zarathustra. Rudolf Steiner tells us that Pythagoras was reborn as one of the Three Wise Men of the East and ultimately became one of the initiated disciples of Jesus of Nazareth.* Zarathustra, through Zarates, points to the highest Sun-Being which descended to the earth, and the transformation of the earth into a sun-filled future planet. This was the path on which this teacher led humanity.

Buddha was the name of the initiate who taught the Mysteries of the Black Sea in his spirit-body. In the sixth century before Christ he was incarnated as *Gautama Buddha*. He rose in his twenty-ninth year from the rank of Bodhisattva to that of Buddha. He no longer appears on earth in physical incarnation but he continues to work for the earth in sending down his influence from the spiritual world. For the more advanced pupils and neophytes in this centre of initiation, it was possible to receive instructions from one who teaches in his etheric body. These pupils were grouped according to their maturity into two unequal divisions, and only the more advanced were chosen for the smaller division. This small group of initiates, who also were endowed with deep humility, endeavoured to receive the *Christ Impulse* to an advanced degree. They became the specially chosen followers of St Paul and received the Christ Impulse directly in the manner St Paul himself had, on the road to Damascus. Thus Buddhism continued and was able to influence not only Asiatic life but also in a certain way those who were imbued with the Christ Impulse in Europe. In Europe the great teachings of Buddha were particularly acceptable to the population because the people were accustomed to the idea of the equality of all human beings (as opposed to the 'caste' order of the East).

The pupils and neophytes who had gained only the Buddha Impulse became the teachers of *equality* and *the brotherhood of man* in Europe. The other group who had additionally received the Christ Impulse considered it their chief task to work especially

---

* Rudolf Steiner, *From Buddha to Christ* (New York, Anthroposophic Press, 1987)

through moral powers. The moral forces worked so strongly that they could purify Europe from the substances of the old 'disease-demons' which had swept through Europe since Attila with his hordes of Huns had invaded.[3] This is a striking example of how moral power enters man and how it must be understood as something quite special. It was originally present in man when his astral body radiated in the golden light of the sun as the Golden Fleece. But man's descent to earth had tarnished the pure gold of the astral body. Now through the Christ Impulse and the working of a strengthened 'I' or Ego in man, humanity is on the ascent again. This strong moral tenet permeated the Mysteries of the Black Sea and was represented through the greatest initiated teacher: Scythianos.

Scythianos was a highly developed individual of ancient times. In later incarnations he became the teacher of the esoteric schools of Europe preparing the Rose Cross Mysteries.[4] As a grand Master builder he was the divine keeper of the Seal related to the Mysteries of the Temple—the physical body of man. Rudolf Steiner tells us in *The East in the Light of the West*[*] of Scythianos as the deeply hidden initiate who preserved the primeval Atlantean wisdom in ancient Europe; a wisdom which penetrated deeply, even into the physical body. They are the ultimate mysteries—of death and the resurrection and of the passage through eternity. Scythianos, among the hidden initiates in Europe, was even more hidden than they, yet he brought into being that esoteric stream which is public and open as well. Since the Mystery of Golgotha and the renting of the veil before the Holiest of the Holies, everything that was hidden before came now out into the open for all men to see and to ponder on.

As was already described at the beginning, through the impulse of one of the most significant conferences in the spirit world three of the greatest initiates reflected downward from the spiritual world. They were called together by a fourth, even greater than they. This individuality is Manes, the highest messenger of the Christ. He called these three together to consult with them how the wisdom which had lived through the post-Atlantean times might gradually come to life again and unfold ever more gloriously

* Rudolf Steiner, *The East in the Light of the West* (New York, Spiritual Science Library, 1986)

into the future. The plan for the future evolution of earthly civilization, which was then decided, was preserved and carried over into those mysteries which are known as the *Rosicrucian Mysteries*. Yet the task of Scythianos was much more comprehensive. He found that the ground on which seeds of wisdom were to be sown was corroded by evil and he knew that human thoughts would gradually lose their divine cosmic origin and serve deepest materialism, egotism and greed. But he also knew that only through love and deep compassion was a salvation of the evil possible. Here he followed his great teacher and leader Manes, who stood over these three initiates as the representative of the 'I' or Ego (which is always closely linked up with the evil, see *The Lord's Prayer*°). The Manichean stream has to do with the fundamental realities of good and evil, and its high aim is not to cast the evil out, but to transform it into good. This *moral* impulse then permeated the western world. Morality is a divine gift given to man in the beginning before his deepest descent. Later it became submerged by the gradual descent of civilisations.

According to Plato the first virtue is wisdom, and he who does not strive for wisdom is not *moral*. The gods once gave wisdom to the unconscious human soul, so that it possessed this wisdom instinctively. But in our age, that of the fifth post-Atlantean epoch, we must work and endeavour to make this knowledge conscious. Through the spiritual science of Anthroposophy we realise that the ideas which are imparted to us are really something divine upon which we are allowed to reflect. We realise that the world has been ordered according to these divine thoughts. When we see Anthroposophy in this respect we will understand that it has been given so that we may be able to fulfil our mission. To this aim we must know how the three initiate teachers, with the fourth above them, had once acted so that we can find a renewal of the impulses of the Mysteries of the Black Sea: the *light of wisdom* through Zaratas; the *equality of human brotherhood* through Buddha; and the *healing power of the progressive good to transform evil* through Scythianos and the Manicheans.

Above them and uniting them is the flaming torch of Manes, pointing far into the future.

° Rudolf Steiner, *The Lord's Prayer* (New York, Anthroposophic Press, 1985)

3
Christian Rosenkreutz and the
Maitreya Buddha

It should be quite obvious to us that the fundamental impulses of spiritual science must find their way into the culture of the present age; and we know too that the culture of the West presents difficulties; so we have to bear in mind how these difficulties arose. We have often heard that there are great differences between successive periods of culture and today we shall speak in closer detail of an extremely important period: the thirteenth century.

Today we can ask where the beginning of the darkness was, which over-shadowed our evolution. Such a point occurred in the thirteenth century when spiritual darkness fell for a time upon all human beings, even the most enlightened, and also upon the initiates. It was there, a moment in time, when the ancient clairvoyance dwindled and no light was shed as direct vision of the spiritual world.

In a deeply moving way, in an art form, this fact found its memorable expression. There was at that point of darkness a 'Contest of singers at the Wartburg'. This was the historical counter image on earth of monumental decisions of the great leading spirits of humanity. In that 'contest' there were some singers who mourned in their songs the inevitable darkness, and there were others who anticipated our modern age; the dominant faculty of forming thoughts instead of 'direct perception' as was the case in Greek times, and in the early stages of our own time.

Among the singers at this 'contest' were those who had still retained some of the old clairvoyance and the most exalted among them was Wolfram von Eschenbach.

And then there were others, more forward looking ones who had lost this ancient bond with the spiritual world and now lived as 'spirit-forsaken'; modern men under the influence of the evil tempting spirits like Klingsor, a luciferic being from Hungary. He got hold of the already 'fallen' soul of the singer Heinrich von Offerdingen, the rival of Wolfram. This is such an incisive moment in the successive epochs of culture, and this turning point is caught in Richard Wagner's opera *Tannhäuser*, the contest of singers at the Wartburg. We hear Wolfram von Eschenbach's valedictory incantation to Venus, the evening star soon setting and allowing darkness to prevail, and his rival Heinrich von Offerdingen bursting out jubilantly in praise of the pleasures of earthly Venus, the source of lust. Reconciling these two as a third element is Elisabeth of Thuringia, called the Holy One, who intervenes and brings redemption to both of them: the one still adhering to the past; the other not yet prepared for the pitfalls of the future.

Precisely at this moment of darkness in the thirteenth century was it necessary for especially suitable personalities to be chosen for initiation; to work into the future once that period of darkness had passed. At this dawn of occultism in the modern age twelve men of deep spirituality came together in order to further the progress of humanity. Of these twelve, seven were embodied as the ancient primeval wise teachers of humanity, the Seven Holy Rishis of the ancient Indian civilisation. These seven were incarnated again in the thirteenth century and were joined by four others who looked back to what mankind had acquired during the four post-Atlantean cultures: 1. Ancient Indian 2. Ancient Persian 3. Egypto-Chaldean 4. Greco-Latin. These four joined the 'college' of the Seven Wise Men in the thirteenth century. The fifth and last of the twelve was more intrinsically intellectual than the rest and it was his task to cultivate and foster external sciences.

Thus there were twelve outstanding individualities and a thirteenth, who was to be chosen out of the kind of initiation demanded by the culture of the West. It was known to the college of the twelve wise men that a child was to be born who possessed great powers of heart and a quality of deep *inward love*, which circumstances had helped to unfold in him. An individuality of extraordinary spirituality was incarnated in this child which also bore within him the Christ Impulse. It was necessary for this child to be removed from the environment into which he was born and to be placed in the care of the twelve at a certain place in Europe not known to us.

Then, at the time when the child had grown into a young man of about 20, he was able to give expression to what was a kind of reflex of the twelve streams of wisdom—but in an altogether *new* form, new even to the twelve wise men. But his metamorphosis was accompanied by violent organic changes within the young man. Even physically this child had to be quite unlike other human beings, he was often very ill and his body became transparent as though filled with light. Then there came a time when his soul departed altogether from his body. The young man lay as if dead. And when his soul returned he spoke of entirely new experiences as if the twelve streams of wisdom were born anew.

He spoke of his own experience similar to that of St Paul before Damascus, and it was through this experience that he could gather together the twelve basic world conceptions into one whole which could do justice to them all. It remains now to be said that the young man died very soon afterwards. His mission had been to create a synthesis of the twelve streams of wisdom in the sphere of thought and to bring forth a new impulse which he then could bequeath to the twelve wise men to carry further. A great and significant impetus had been given. The name of the individuality from whom this impulse originated was Christian Rosenkreutz.[5]

The same individuality was born again in the fourteenth century and this earthly life lasted more than a hundred years. In this new earthly life he brought fruitfulness to the outer world too. He travelled all over the west (under the name of Count St Germain) and practically the whole of the then known world in order to receive anew the wisdom as a kind of essence which was to filter into the culture of the times. Again he came to Damascus and had St Paul's experience for a second time. This experience is to be regarded as the fruit of the seed which had been laid in the preceding incarnation. All the forces of his exceptional etheric body remained intact after death and did not dissolve in the ether world.

Because every century in our civilisation tends towards something new and also imparts it into the stream of evolution, this great spiritual leader of humanity Christian Rosenkreutz is reincarnated every hundred years. His reincarnation in the sixteenth century and then again in the twentieth century seem to be of the greatest significance.

For the sake of a clear conception of the future evolution of humanity we shall concentrate on the deeds of Christian Rosen-kreutz in the sixteenth and beginning of the seventeenth century. For this purpose I have lead you back to the Mystery centre which we know already from previous visits. It is the centre of initiation at Colchis in the neighbourhood of the Black Sea in which great leaders of humanity taught, including Buddha in his spirit body from whom more advanced pupils received instructions, and an individuality who centuries later lived in a physical body and is known to us as St Francis of Assisi.

Towards the end of the sixteenth century there took place an occult conference of great leading individualities associated with Christian Rosenkreutz. The individuality who in the sixth century before Christ had been incarnated as Gautama Buddha also participated.

With this meeting of Christian Rosenkreutz with the Buddha we touch upon an Eastern element, that of karma and reincarna-tion in the esoteric teachings of the Buddha i.e. that our karma must be directed away from earth, away from sickness, death, from passion and desires, so that future reincarnations on the earth are of no more importance. The cleansed soul is entering *Nirvana*.

The Rosicrucian initiation of previous centuries had to be modified again in our time. A new element entered the spiritual stream which could not have entered into it in previous centuries. The teaching of reincarnation and karma must today stand at the very starting point of spiritual knowledge which was not possible in previous centuries and therefore did not enter the Rosicrucian initiation. This initiation in the twentieth century reveals that after a certain period after death the human soul has to enter a region for purification in the soul world. Before the soul enters this region, known to spiritual science as *Kamaloka*, the individ-ual experiences the meeting with a quite definite Being who presents him with his karmic account, and for a great number of men this judge of our karmic accounts once had the form of Moses. Hence the medieval formula which originated in Rosicru-cianism: Moses presents man in the hour of his death with the register of his sins and at the same time points to the 'stern law'.

This showed man how much he had departed from the stern law according to which he should have acted. In the course of our period however this office passes over to Christ Jesus—a significant point—and will do so more and more in the future. Man will meet Christ Jesus as his Judge after death; that is to say the ordering of karmic transactions will in future happen through Christ. More and more men of the future will feel: 'I am going through the gate of death with my karmic account; on the one side stand my good, clever and beautiful deeds—my clever, beautiful, good and intelligent thoughts—on the other side stand everything evil, wicked, stupid, foolish and loathsome'. But He who in the future will have the office of Judge, for the incarnations in the evolution of humanity, will bring order into this karmic account of man. This is the *deed of the Christ.* Events will happen which will not only balance the karmic account of each individual but in the best possible way fit in with the general concerns of the whole world. We must so balance our karma that we can help in the best possible manner the forward progress of the whole human race on earth. It was necessary in human evolution that souls should first accept the Christ Impulse, so that the thought of reincarnation might enter into human consciousness in a ripe form.

The Bodhisattvas

The loftiest teachers of successive epochs are the Bodhisattvas who already in the pre-Christian era pointed to Christ in his full reality. One of these pre-Christian Bodhisattvas was born as the son of a king in India 550 years before Christ, lived and taught for 29 years as a Bodhisattva and then ascended to the rank of Buddha. Such an individuality does not incarnate again in a physical body on earth. An ancient phase of evolution came to a conclusion with the attainment of Buddhahood by the Bodhisattva. When a Bodhisattva becomes a Buddha he hands the crown of his office to the new Bodhisattva who succeeds him. This new Bodhisattva had a particular mission to fulfil in the history of mankind. The task allotted to him was the spiritual guidance of the movement represented in the doctrines of the Therapeutae and Essenes.[6] During the early post-Christian era, about 105 BC, a certain individuality was sent by this Bodhisattva into the communities of the Essenes to be their guide and leader. He was an incarnation of the new Bodhisattva. His name was Jeshu Ben Pandira, as known in the Talmudist literature. He was a great and noble personality; a herald of Christianity among the Essenes. But he had great enemies and was accused of blasphemy and heresy. He was stoned and his corpse suspended on a cross. A hundred years before the Mystery of Golgotha, through Jeshu ben Pandira, an essential spiritual mission was carried out—the preparation for the coming of Christ in the etheric.[7]

In Jeshu ben Pandira we see a personality standing under the *guardianship of the present Bodhisattva*. A new stream—additional to the main Christian stream—originated from the Buddha's successor, the present Bodhisattva (who later on will become the Maitreya Buddha, and who sent his emissary into the Essene communities where he executed his mission).

So far we have mentioned the Bodhisattva who became Buddha about 600 BC and the successive Bodhisattva who is to work for the future Christ event. But something important must be said concerning the reincarnation of the Bodhisattva and how and when he may be recognised as such in his reincarnation. It is of great significance that a great transformation must take place in the life of a reincarnated Bodhisattva. He is never recognised as such as a child, or in his youth, even if he were an exceptionally gifted child. The great transformation takes place between the thirtieth and thirty-first year when the personality of a Bodhisattva descends to bring new forces for the evolution of humanity. This change never shows itself in youth. The distinctive feature is precisely that the later years are so totally unlike the youthful ones.

The Bodhisattva of our time prepared himself for this incarnation so that he may appear and may rise to the dignity of the Buddha in 3000 years hence; looking back on all that has happened in the new epoch and on the Christ Impulse and all that is connected with it. This Bodhisattva prepared himself to be able not only to hear the teaching of compassion and love through inspiration from above, but to look *within* and hear that teaching as *the voice of his own heart*. This was the case with the ancient Buddha and his illumination under the Bodhi Tree. Compassion and love sprang up within his own heart and there arose a quality in the human soul which others could then follow. It is so with every human capacity; first one individual develops it within himself and then others can follow. As time goes on, more and more people will be able to find this within themselves and at about AD 3000 there will be a sufficient number of people living on earth who will have developed in their own hearts what the present Bodhisattva has prepared. All the preparations today are connected with the fact that men are drawing nearer and nearer to an ideal in the West, and the whole direction of inner evolution in future times will be that the ideas which we hold of the Good are also immediately *moral impulses*. That will be the direction of the evolution which we shall experience in the times that are approaching.

In the following centuries and millenia speech will acquire an unexpected effect, and in the coming 3000 years everything intellectual will at the same time be *moral* and that which is moral will penetrate *into the hearts of men*. In the next 3000 years the human race must become permeated with 'magic morality', otherwise the human race will not be able to bear such an evolution, it will only misuse it. Only then will it be possible that, 3000 years after our present time, the Bodhisattva of the twentieth century will become the Maitreya Buddha, and the stream going forth from the Maitreya Buddha will unite with the stream of Western spiritual life connected with Christian Rosenkreutz. It is the mission of the Maitreya Buddha to prepare human beings for the epoch connected mainly with the development of *true morality*, and the words of his speech will contain the magic power of the Good. The Maitreya Buddha will be a bringer of love and compassion by way of the 'Word', the Logos. He will then be able to teach mankind the Christ Impulse, and in that age the Buddha stream and the Christ stream will flow into one. Only so can the Christ Mystery be truly understood.

For anyone who follows the descriptions of the two spiritual streams of Christian Rosenkreutz and the Maitreya Buddha, a question inevitably arises: How are we to recognise the task of Anthroposophy on behalf of mankind?

'Anthroposophy', Rudolf Steiner said, 'is the spiritual science of today'. It embraces a far wider sphere than that known to Rosicrucianism (which did not yet include insight into reincarnation and karma).

Without this fundamental knowledge of the continuity of destiny throughout the course of various lives it would not have been possible to grasp the nature and being of Christian Rosenkreutz. And on the other hand there would also have been no understanding for the spiritual movement connected with the secret of the future Maitreya Buddha's incarnation.

Rosicrucianism holds the Christ event holy in the most *intimate inwardness* on the one hand, and on the other hand recognises the Maitreya Buddha, the *Bringer of Goodness*, who will develop into the greatest martyr of the Golgotha Mystery. These two streams, which spring from different sources, have now united themselves in a common task.

Where has this alliance become a modern event? When did this union begin to show itself to be effective? Within the initiate consciousness of Rudolf Steiner, and through the word and deed of Anthroposophy which proclaims it.

Here the reality of the brotherly union in the spirit is consumated. And so it becomes the call, the summons to a new revelation of the Christ event, which in the light of re-embodiment and destiny deepens and becomes inward in a hitherto unknown form within the consciousness of mankind.

4
Manicheism Today

When we embark on an investigation of Manicheism according to the documents and records, we have to discriminate between the material itself and its author. Confronted with such documentation the general questions arises: Is it the subject-matter or the author who speaks?

To avoid this predicament, this study of Mani his life and his teaching is based more on mystery wisdom, handed down throughout the centuries, and relies only to a certain extent on historical documentation. Before we investigate what Manicheism is 'about' let us consider first of all its founder Manes or Mani. Tradition has it that he chose his own name (as a child he was called Corbicius). With this choice he likewise proclaimed his goal. Mani—Manes—Manus—Manu; this name always points to a mankind which is not of earthly but of heavenly, cosmic origin. Mani himself still possessed this cosmic knowledge in his art, his teaching, his cult, but permeated throughout by the Ego consciousness. He intended to make accessible to every man what in former times was working in humanity as a whole; the cosmic forces. As this name Mani is manifold like those of other initiates (for example Zarathustra) general information from history is chaotic and contradictory. The tradition, especially that of the Middle Ages, shows two aberrations. The 'Oriental sources' are inclined to be *fantastic*, and the 'Western sources' with their stringent, dogmatic thinking, confine the tradition to the *confessional*.

But what does mystery wisdom convey? The name of Mani's father was Scythianos, which indicates that he was a man who carried the name of his people. The Scythians were a nomad race, well known to ancient writers. He adopted the name Scythianos as his own because he united within him their whole wisdom. To carry the name of one's people was a grade of initiation. Christ said of Nathanael: 'Behold an Israelite indeed, in whom is no guile.' (St John 1:4). Scythianos had a prisoner as a wife who persuaded him to wander from the wilderness to Egypt where he came into contact with the Mystery centres there. After some time he intended to travel to Jerusalem, but he died on the journey. After his death Scythianos' writings came into the hands of a widow and from her passed on to Mani who also became her foster child at the age of seven. When she died Mani was twelve years old and at this age had his first spiritual encounter with the Angel El Tawam, who pointed out to him his own special mission and admonished him to leave his inherited religion which was Persian. (See Albert Steffen's *The Death Experience of Manes**, Act 2.) The Angel El Tawam's realm was the sphere of the Sun. He was considered as one of the hosts of Michael (in some ancient records even that of Michael himself in pre-christian times).

When Mani was 24 years old he confronted King Shapur I on the day of his coronation and proclaimed himself as a spiritual leader. Shapur intended to destroy him but at the persuasion of his wife Nadhira, Mani was called to the court at Ghondi-Shapur as tutor to the King's eldest son. When the boy fell ill Mani offered his healing gifts to save the boy's life. But he failed and the boy died. Mani was consequently imprisoned. (See the historical records collected and edited by O.G. von Wesendonk,[8] which received high recognition.)

But the spiritual reason why Mani could not save the prince's life was realised by him in a vision or deep meditation. Between the statues of Buddha and Zarathustra Mani beholds himself as the 'Youth of Nain'. Christ appears, comforts the mother, touches the bier and the youth arises from the bonds of death. From this spiritual experience Mani learns that he could not heal the child because his own soul was not yet awakened by Christ. It inspired Mani to deepen his teaching more and more with the coming Christianity so that his disciples would be better equipped to give the world a *new* message.

When King Shapur saw his state religion endangered he condemned Mani to death. Mani escaped to the castle Arabion, and from there to Kaskar in Mesopotamia. Here he encountered

* Albert Steffen, *The Death Experience of Manes* (New York, Folder Editions, 1970)

the Christian bishop Archelaus with whom he had a dogmatic argument on Christianity. Mani refused to accept the bishop's dogma and was banned by a religious council. Again he was forced to save his life and fled to Khatai in China and founded Christian communities everywhere.

After the death of King Shapur, Mani returned to the Persian capital. He had gone through many mystery experiences. He was a conqueror in spirit, accomplished as a human being, teacher, artist and great painter. But the successor of King Shapur, his son Barahm I, was as hostile as his father and called Mani before a synod of Persian priests and scholars who demanded that Mani should recant Christianity. When he refused he was condemned to death in AD 277. His decapitated body was skinned and the skin filled with precious herbs. It was then crucified before the gates of Ghondi-Shapur as a sign of admonition.

What are the symptoms for such an initiate's destiny? As we heard at the beginning, Mani was called the 'Son of a Widow', a mystery designation from ancient Egypt. In the Egyptian mystery wisdom Isis, the image of the soul, seeks for Osiris in her wanderings on earth to unify his dismembered body. The soul has lost its original relationship with the cosmos. Horus was born as the 'Son of the Widow' whom Isis had spiritually conceived. Both, the Youth of Nain and Parsifal, like Mani, had this designation. It conveys that the Ego, the child of the soul, has lost the father, i.e. the ground of the world, and has to create this being within itself out of freedom and love.

Mani had received the whole mystery wisdom since the Atlantis Flood.[9] He survived the flood and as Manu, the Noah of Genesis, was the founder of the Seven Root-Races.[10] He united within his being the Indian and the Egypto-Chaldean cultures and unified them with his own, the Persian culture. But this ancient wisdom did not suffice. He had to renew it and penetrate it with the power of the Christ Impulse, so that he could become the healer of humanity from the forces of darkness.

To understand Manicheism and its attitude to the forces of evil in man and in the world, it is advisable to study the writings of the opponents of Manicheism, especially those of St Augustine the Church-father. Augustine's opposition stemmed from the fact that he was unable to overcome the dark element within himself. His faith, enhanced and enflamed through an immeasurable devotion (*Credo Quia Absurdum*) finds its passionate expression in his *Confessions*. They strike us as a divine dithyramb of a modern man, an egobearer, who has renounced knowledge. Tortured by unanswerable questions, Augustine wrestles with the problem of pre-existence. He cannot behold the divine with his senses anymore, as the Greeks could, and he rejects the 'Ten Categories of Aristotle' which he knew since his youth. In his state of self torture he comes to the conclusion that not all men are destined to come to God and to attain immortaility through freedom. The others are outcasts who remain in sin: in an *abyss of darkness* they are doomed.

It is precisely this belief of Augustine's which differs from Manicheism, and which led him to its persecution. Mani, to him, was a heretic. Whereas Augustine beheld a good and an evil state of mankind, forever separated, Mani realised that those forces which are good need to be used for the transformation and the redemption of evil.

The Manicheans saw in the *search for the evil itself* the beginning of the transformation. This search was an *act of cognition*. What is the origin of evil? Evil is in the first place a displaced good. What in one sphere or at one time is right and good is evil in another sphere or at another time. Mani came to the shattering conclusion that however far he investigated the origin of sin, he could detect no being in it. The Creator, the Spirit of Light, can only bring forth a good creation. Therefore darkness and evil must arise out of the reversal of the will of the highest being through man who has turned away from this divine will to exert only his own base one.

Here gapes the abyss which separates modern man from his divine origin. Modern man, since the fifteenth century is so organised that an abyss yawns between his sense-organisation and the spirit which permeates the world. Only a thinking which is freed from the mirror of the bodily brain can ever bridge the abyss and cast light into the darkness. It is here where *fear* rears its head because, unconsciously, humanity stands at the threshold of the abyss.

But this attitude changes as soon as man recognises the *reincarnation* of his *eternal entelechy* or being. Reincarnation was part of Manichean teaching and is historically documented in the works of O.G. von Wesendonk on Manicheism, a respected research on which Albert Steffen also drew as a source for his writings about Mani.

The Manicheans believed that in the course of repeated earth-lives the light will be victorious over the darkness, in a process of gradual soul transformation. Man will become a co-fighter of the King of Light against the Regent of Darkness. But this fight is an entirely individual one and demands courage instead of fear. In the course of repeated earth-lives man need not cast off the evil and surrender it to eternal perdition, but to gradually transform it and make it transparent. Only he who can look upon his errors again and again, and with *objective observation* correct them, will ultimately find the origin of evil. In a creative process the interplay of Light and Darkness will appear as colour. Man does not only experience in black and white as Augustine did, but in the living colours of the rainbow. Mani himself was known as a painter and he spread his teachings through paintings rather than words. He had overcome the weight of the dark earth through the weight-less nature of the light in its twofold meaning: as the absence of darkness and as anti-gravity. Mani had already etherised his blood[11] (which carries egotism) and had thus become a Manus bearer of the spirit-self.

But Mani saw his task not only in the transformation of his own self, but of the whole earth. Earth must become a Light body again and he spoke of a future Terra Lucida. (Christian Morgenstern, the great German poet of our time, expressed the same idea in the words: 'That she [the earth] too might become a sun'—'*Dass auch sie einst Sonne werde*'.)

Mani had the experience of the Mystery of Golgotha and with it the transformation of the earth, independent and irrespective of the historical event. In his spiritual awareness he recognised it as a 'mystical fact'. His Ego was purified of everything appertaining to the body. Light and darkness were neither good nor evil, but the deeds and sufferings of the gods. He was in this sense a forerunner of Goethe whose theory of colour* is based on the certainty that colour is the balance of light and darkness. Goethe attributes these deeds and sufferings to the Elohim. Where and when

* Johann Wolfgang von Goethe, *Theory of Colours* (London, John Murray, 1840). Extracts also appear in *Goethe's Approach to Colour*, edited by John Fletcher (Mercury Arts Publications, 1987)

darkness prevails the light is suffering. In this sense Goethe called the impact and experience of colour 'sense-moral'.

Through his mystery schooling Mani had comprehended the various stages of the earth through world evolution. Why has darkness got hold of the earth? How did this dark age come about? Night entered into it when the earth became a solid and impenetrable body. Earth does not let the light filter through, earth itself is dark. Darkness might be considered as absence of light in various degrees. But the varying potency of darkness is more than mere absence of light. Darkness is a being, a regent. It is the counterpart, an opposing creator of a 'counter-earth'. Other elements also became heavier and denser through the condition of matter. Water and air are heavier, and light is diffused and becomes electricity.

The 'counter-earth' is thus the result of a gradual densification of the elements. Augustine was fully aware of the dark, polluted, densified state of the earth and rightly called it: *Terra Pestifera*, forever void of light, forever doomed.

Against it stands Mani's true cognition of the Resurrected Christ who took the darkness of the *Terra Pestifera* into a Light-Earth. Before his resurrection Christ entered the *Terra Pestifera* or Hell and in his infinite compassion helped to take this darkness into light. This resurrected Light-Earth Mani named *Terra Lucida*, a future state of humanity.

Before the assault of the Spirit of Darkness the earth consisted of pure water (life), pure air (breath of God) and fire (purified will).

These were the aeons in which divine spiritual beings existed. Mani intended to create this *Terra Lucida* as a future abode of humanity. It is the ultimate goal for a transformation into light through freedom and love; not to turn away from evil, not to cast it out but 'to love the evil good'. That is the ultimate message of true Manicheism.

Manicheism is a future stage of humanity, the age of the Holy Spirit, the age of generations who have transformed the astral body into the spirit-self or Manas. That Mani is the representative of this Spirit-Age is clearly indicated at the end of Albert Steffen's *The Death Experience of Manes*. Manes has helped the Jew Nicanor to freedom.

Manes: 'O Nicanor, have you not thrown aside darkness? Go, I set you free.'

Nicanor: 'Then joyfully, as free man I behold you, the spirit of truth, O Manes, thou comforter!'

This is the word which Christ used at his Ascension: I shall send you the *comforter* which is the Holy Spirit.

5
The Three Kings

I had quite a serious battle with my conscience about whether to find a totally new concept and representation for the Three Kings or to retain their golden glory of the past (as we see them depicted by painters of the Middle Ages and the Renaissance in all the beauty of glowing reds, soft greens, chaste blues and flaming gold). 'No' said my conscience finally, 'beauty without truth is an illusion.' So I transplanted the Three Kings into the present time with its atomic threats, with its fears, with its poverty, with the homelessness of most of mankind and its spiritual and physical hunger. I was actually curious to see how they would emerge out of these grim conditions. This is what my talk is about.

The Christmas annunciation which is heralded by the angels to mankind is threefold. It speaks of a revelation of divine powers on high of 'peace on earth' and of 'men of good will'. This message, which encompasses all races, all people and individualities, today appears to have wholly died away.

Revelation as such has become *dogma*. Revelation presupposes belief and this can no longer be a criterion for the man of our time, attuned to natural science and sub-natural electronics and motivated by technology. The name of God, which still remains the last vestige of revelation, no longer has any tangible spiritual reality and appears not to be 'opportune' for future peace on earth, which seems to be guaranteed by nuclear weapons. The 'tidings of great joy' which shall be to all people, of which the Gospel of St Luke tells, can no longer be spoken of today. And the call of the Angeloi 'fear not' has turned into the opposite. Peace, it is thought, can only be achieved through fear of the atom bomb, or the still more terrible gifts of mechanised science. Indeed to speak at all of 'good will among men' has become meaningless. For such a will, if it is not to remain blind and in its blindness to sow harm, must be founded upon the *knowledge* of the spiritual world. But this is simply put aside.

Both God without revelation and goodwill without knowledge lead to sectarianism, only with different signatures; here passive, there active—never however to a peace on earth encompassing all people, but only to further estrangement, to a new conflict and eventually to complete chaos.

People today are still very far from directing a keen knowing look upon the earth as a whole, in spite of all education in the understanding of wildlife and the life and behaviour of nature. They see in this planet, which they can encircle in a few days by aeroplane, only a dead organism composed of the physical substances of already known or not yet known elements; a mineral cosmic body. Over its cooled crust the plant kingdom, moss, grass, trees, etc. spreads itself; the animal kingdom moves and human cultures rise and fall. The whole is headed for a general death which is more or less retarded or hastened by the activities of man, by the sciences or arts in their rise or decline, so that to the natural catastrophies which can be foreseen cultural breakdowns are added (of which we are experiencing a deadly foretaste). This apocalyptic prognosis enters ever more into the consciousness of humanity and spreads a panic of terror.

Out of this total darkness, which only comprehends destruction and self-destruction, a glimmer of light giving a different direction is seen: the direction toward a spiritual-scientific knowledge and another view of the world by which the earth organism in its entirety is revealed. It is spiritual revelation whereby the earth organism becomes a breathing, ensouled entity infused with spirit.

Each human being is an 'atlas'. In his bodily organism he bears the entire earth within him. It makes an enormous difference whether he conceives the earth organism as something dead or as being alive, ensouled and spirit-filled. At birth he is laden with his 'portion of earth' and at death he casts it from him again. When he consumes the material substance of the earth, or takes it into himself in a more rarefied form in his breathing or through his senses, man is a being who towers above the kingdom of nature and organises it himself. He draws substances into his own human realm.

In this way man can *transubstantiate* the substances of the earth which he takes into himself through the warmth of his metabolic system, and where warmth arises his soul and spirit now take hold. The substances of nature are thus transmuted into an inner fire of a moral quality; through a moral thought, through the enthusiasm of the soul, through the inner fire for a spiritual goal. It can kindle this warmth through which natural substances become human, and as his final goal man can humanize the whole earth, so that when he dies he can give it back to the cosmos in another form than that in which it had been received at birth. Through imprinting the stamp of his spirit upon everything of a natural order man has to exercise a creative activity. This creative activity enables him out of his own freedom to take his place within earthly creation. Man is appointed to continue the work of the Creator. 'Ye are Gods' said Christ to his disciples and these words can only make sense if man becomes a creator. This is his highest dignity and the revelation of the Mysteries in our time. Through Christ's union with the earth the resurrected man inhabits the temple where, before, the gods rested.

But these revelations fade away and we must go back in time to the beginning of the fifteenth century when the natural-scientific conception of the world, based upon sense perception and the intellect, was accepted as standard. What remains are laws which are expressed in numbers. The ever more widespread material sciences are supplemented by astro-physical and astro-chemical formulae. All that has taken shape upon the earth as an ancient wisdom in the most manifold spiritual centres—the last traces of the Mysteries on the various continents—have lost their meaning. Finally only what is useful technologically remains.

The flyer who encircles the earth in his aeroplane and looks down upon its surface, does not have the experience of the wanderer who went on a pilgrimage from one centre of culture to another (as was the custom among the ancients, in order to experience ever and again new stages of initiation). Not merely space but also time now becomes for him bereft of soul. Whether he looks out into the reaches of space or back down the march of time, he finds as a final end or as a beginning only nothingness. He races into a void. On the other hand one who glides along in a flying machine, who looks out into the azure blue of the sky and *gives himself up to it with his soul* does not remain devoid of feeling. A sense of devotion can even here become tangibly alive.

As he flies into the glow of the setting sun his fearless quest for knowledge and his moral will can gather strength.

One summer evening, flying back from Dornach, Switzerland, it was as if the aeroplane was dipping right into a glowing sunset over the waters of the channel. All colours seemed to have been intensified and inwardly deepened: blue to violet and yellow to orange. Perception had freed itself from the fetters of the body and a sentient experience became at the same time a moral one. Through this kind of seeing man undergoes a catharsis; his Ego is no longer cleaved to his perishable body, which weighs him down, but unites itself with the weightless body which is in the becoming. He leads the earth on towards a higher state of existence. His final motif is transfiguration.

These are experiences which arise when the consciousness soul of man is transformed into the imaginative soul, a metamorphosis which occurs when man treads the path from the spirit within him to the spirit in the cosmos; to sun, moon and stars and finally a harmonious survey of destiny. This is the goal of the Mysteries of our time, as knowingly revealed through Anthroposophy.

There was a series of very enlightening articles published in the weekly publication *Das Goetheanum*.[12] Here we read that Johann Kepler, the great astronomer of Prague, had very profound ideas about various constellations, even before the time of Christ. The most important one however was the one in his own time around the year 1604: the great conjunction of Jupiter and Saturn in Scorpio. Johann Kepler had very deep thoughts about this constellation together with another especially radiant star which originally he thought to be Mars, but this theory was soon discarded and the radiant source of light received the name 'Stella Nova' (the New Star). In one of the above mentioned articles in *Das Goetheanum*, Suso Vetter writes about the 'Stella Nova' and the year 1604 and he relates the following:

> 'English astronomers discovered that at the time of the birth of Christ the astronomy of the Far East had arrived at a much higher level of knowledge than that of Europe. They investigated the astronomical research works and discovered that as early as about 500 BC Chinese astronomers recorded the sight of a new star of great radiance and

at about 400 BC Korean astronomers also reported the sight of a radiant star within the conjunction of Jupiter and Saturn which was visible for a considerable length of time. It was already foretold that this 'nova' will light and guide the path of the Three Magi or Magos, to the birthplace of the Saviour to come. These traditions were gradually handed down through the ages and most certainly came into the hands of Johann Kepler (1571-1630).

He was the first to make very exact astronomical calculations, based on investigations of Tycho de Brahe who had already worked on them thoroughly for decades. Thus Kepler discovered a threefold conjunction of Jupiter and Saturn joined by Mars somewhat later. Very soon Kepler was startled by the discovery that in the year 1604 a new star, and not Mars, shone radiantly over the conjunction for which he too adopted the term 'Nova'. Kepler in his writings then referred to a Divine Providence in so far as God himself announced the birth of His Son, the Christ, through a shining star out of this conjunction and that, through its intervention the Three Magi were led to the land of Israel and to its little town of Bethlehem, to the crib of the newly born King of the Jews. Also Chaldaean records had transmitted the knowledge that at the times of such great conjunctions extraordinary people are born. Kepler must have accepted these findings and it dawned in his soul, which was so deeply immersed in the harmonic relationship of the starry realms to earth and humanity, something which Rudolf Steiner expressed in these words: "In epochs in which, as it were, gods wish to work from the astral world into the etheric world such a phenomenon as a quickly radiant and quickly fading star becomes visible."' (4, 6, 1924) Rudolf Steiner, *The Festivals and their Meaning*, (London, Rudolf Steiner Press, 1981).

However, ordinary astronomy has never ever heard anything of these occurrences. The Three Kings were never rulers in the ancient sense, nor law givers, nor representatives of a High Order of their race and their people. They are pictured to us as wanderers; as pilgrims in quest of the 'new' that is to come into this world. They look for this 'new', the promised Messiah, in

ancient mystical places but do not find him there. The decline
which cannot be averted has begun. In Herod they recognise a
representative of the will to destruction inherent in a degenerate
Kingship (which was formerly a bearer of divinity).[13] He con-
demns the new generation to death so that by this means he can
do away with the World King. The cradle of the child who is to
become the bearer of the Christ, whose kingdom is not of this
world, stands in *Beth-Lechem* (the house of the Bread). They
continue their journey to him. The Three Kings are representatives of pre-Christian mysteries. As such they had undergone
schooling and received revelations of the spiritual world. They
knew that this ancient 'mystery wisdom' had come to an end with
the coming of Christ and the new mystery wisdom of which they
read in the stars. They find in the Solomon Jesus boy[14] a child of
Jewish parents. This is true, but they are led by the individuality of
that child by the Golden Star, a new star, a 'Stella Nova'. It moves
above their heads and brings to the earth the impulse of freedom
and love to all mankind. A wonderful harmony of race, nations,
folk and individualtiy is the great new Christian mystery.

The Three Wise Men transplanted the ancient mystery wisdom
into the 'beginning' when the Logos was still with God. But they
also wanted to transplant it right into the present that it might
grow and flourish into the future. They wished to place the
cosmic, human impulse of Christ Jesus into the present and thus
inaugurate the post-Christian mysteries. They knew that this was
not possible without transforming the inner life of 'thinking,
feeling and willing' through the Ego, which takes into itself the
Word which has become flesh. Has anything of this goal—we
might ask ourselves—been realised up to the present day?

In the course of the many Epiphany lectures, I have given many
and various aspects of a new and quite different 'thinking, feeling
and willing', especially in connection with the healing acts, the
miracles of the Christ. If I endeavour to do so today it will have to
be as the gifts of the Three Kings, the Wise Men, to humanity. If we
say: 'I think, I feel, I will', three distinct activities of the Ego are
hereby indicated. But the more they are intensified the less they
yield to the penetration of our ordinary consciousness. If I study
the thoughts I have, they are indeed thoughts which *I* have, but
are none the less perhaps not my *own* thoughts. Other people
before me may have thought them. In general man adheres, for

reasons he is seldom conscious, to a particular world conception. He is subject to the 'time spirit'.

Thoughts as such have only then value when they are true for all men. The comprehensive thinker is spread out with his thoughts over the whole world and looks upon himself from the standpoint of mankind. He is, while *thinking*, the macrocosmic man.

When a man *feels*, and tests his *feelings*, they prove to be for the most part that of his *folk* to which he belongs, those of his family or those of his party. They are awakened through contact with the people connected with him. In reality these feelings, which I share with others, are only my own in so far as I widen them to my own Ego experience. Then I shall be able to follow them as joy and pain and suffer them as such with my fellow human beings. But to do so is a *moral* act. Sympathy and antipathy must be transformed into soul organs free of inner influence and outer-fetters. Only then do they belong to our Ego and not to instincts born out of traditions and dreams. Man lives, while feeling, in resounding harmony with the world souls.

And finally in our *will* we discover, only after we have performed a deed, that we have not followed our own individual will. Only too often when we believe we have acted out of our will and intentions, in reality we act not of ourselves but out of our race; out of past loyalties to our forefathers, out of our generation or, religiously speaking, of our God. This happens because as a human being who *wills* man has absolutely no consciousness of himself. Man can feel himself of *good will* only if he endeavours in his own earthly destiny to share the lot of all mankind. He is in accord with his own conscience only when the guiding force of his will is: 'Not I, but the Christ in me.'

True *thinking* is to share thoughts with the whole world. True *feeling* is to share joy and pain with fellow men. True or good *will* is to share in destiny the lot of mankind.

Many a saga tells us of the wise men, Kaspar, Melchior and Balthasar. They are regarded as the guardian saints of travellers and pilgrims. I remember from my childhood days that I saw frequently the letters 'K.M.B.' engraved above the porches of a house, on altar cloths in churches, above shoe-makers' shops; and for a long time I did not know their meaning. Nor was I aware of the Three Kings' names. I also do not recall when I woke up to their meaning—but I knew that it was said that they watch over us that we might not go astray and take a wrong path. They pointed the way into the homeland which can never again be lost.

Today men have become homeless. Whoever may still call a home his own could lose it tomorrow. New world catastrophies, which are already visible on the political horizon, will increase the number of the homeless to an immeasurable degree. And if a man finds a roof he can call his own it is one under which he no longer comes to know himself. He resorts to a computerised existence. In what profession does he really feel himself at home? He is everywhere cast out of his humanity. No profession is a 'professing' or a calling. He joins the ranks of the profession-less, the unemployed.

But let us end with the comforting thought that whoever takes the Three Kings to himself as helpers follows not merely earthly human beings but cosmic human beings, who lead him to his God-created Egohood which passes through birth and death and outlives the end of the earth.

6
Three Awakenings

If I were asked—and I have been asked—'What is so new and exceptional about Anthroposophy?', my answer would be and has been: 'Man as a threefold being'. Anthroposophy, as the name implies should have man as a starting point, and not the hierarchies or the spiritual worlds. To reach beyond we need a firm starting point. In this time, when a great thinker like Bertrand Russell considers man as being merely a higher animal with certain faculties, which has a body and some kind of feeling and a mind, the threefold aspect of man is of paramount importance. In its highest order this threefold conception of man is addressed in the Foundation Stone meditation[15] as head, heart and limbs; the abode of the Holy Trinity.

Another consideration of what is new and exceptional in Anthroposophy is that on the basis of the threefold man concept Rudolf Steiner could speak for the first time about karma and reincarnation in a way appropriate to our time and to Western civilisation (the East has a totally different concept[16] which Rudolf Steiner knew only too well through his relationship with the Theosophical Society).

If we were to investigate all true Rosicrucian teachings throughout the Middle Ages up to the seventeenth century we would see that the concept of karma and reincarnation is nowhere to be found. In these Rosicrucian writings one can find references to alchemy (the transformation of primawateria into quinta essentia, the meaning of salt, water and sulphur, and the transformation of lead to gold). One will find further references to Neo-Platonism and to the Jewish Cabbala and their mystic teachings. It was only Rudolf Steiner whose true Rosicrucian message included karma and reincarnation. As far back as 1910 he gave indications on karma exercises, but after the Christmas

Foundation Meeting,[17] when the Rosicrucian stream united with the Michael Impulse, his revelations about karma and reincarnation found its culmination. The new form of karma exercises allowed research into the reincarnations of many great individualities and the important karmic streams which formed the karma of the Anthroposophical Movement. Rudolf Steiner also stipulated that unless an anthroposophist has discovered the particular stream to which he belongs, karma exercises can be more harmful than furthering.

Our fundamental investigation today is also a threefold one, based on the foundation of Rudolf Steiner's question: 'What became of the Three Wise Men of the East?' Who were they and what did they represent? What was to be awakened in them? It is generally known which gifts the individual kings brought to the Jesus child at Bethlehem. But in his investigations Rudolf Steiner speaks of three seeds which they brought. Through the New Christ Impulse these seeds will grow, flower and bear fruit.

The Three Kings are representative of three past cultural epochs, and it is to the past we have to turn to understand what became of them. The seeds offered to the child were *awakened* by the Christ and bear the forces which can permeate three later cultural epochs with the Christ Impulse. The wisdom of the third post-Atlantean epoch is awakened by the Christ that it may bear fruit in our fifth epoch.

The second post-Atlantean epoch, the epoch of Zarathustra, is awakened so that in the sixth epoch there may come about a true understanding of Christ. And with the help of the Christ Impulse, the first post-Atlantean epoch, that of Ancient India, has its resurrection in the seventh epoch. In each case Christ must awaken a special personality, a human soul suited by destiny to be the bearer of this seed of culture from ancient times and who can see to it that the gifts brought by Christ to mankind are carried onwards, so that a right understanding of the Christ and his mission may be brought to humanity in later epochs.

The 'young man of Nain' and Mani

In the Gospel of St Luke (chapter 7) we are told in moving words of the awakening of the young man of Nain. Every word in this story is full of significance. It indicates how in the young man of Nain there was a living representative of the whole third post-

Atlantean epoch of the Egypto-Chaldean culture, as it had been able to develop under those forces which at that time worked upon the soul of man (this is confirmed in the Gospel of St Matthew 2:15: 'And was there [in Egypt] until the death of Herod: that it might be fulfilled which was spoken of the Lord by the prophet, saying, Out of Egypt have I called my son').

The young man of Nain in St Luke's gospel is none other than the disciple at Sais. We know that he stood before the being who said of himself: I am He who is—who was—and who will be. The disciple of Sais wished, while still unprepared, to become an initiate and lift the veil which 'No mortal can lift'. He wished to become as the other initiates a 'Son of the Widow' of Isis who mourned for her lost spouse, Osiris. Because he wished to unveil the image of Isis as a mortal i.e. to behold in an unprepared state the secrets of the heavens, death came upon him. (It was Novalis who proclaimed: 'Then let us become immortal to lift the veil from the mysteries of the starry realms'.) The wisdom of the Egyptian epoch which has lost its power is symbolised in the Disciple at Sais. He is born again and grows up as the young man of Nain. He is the 'Son of the Widow', and he dies in his youth. Christ Jesus comes near as the dead youth is being carried through the gates of the city. Many people are there, including the youth's mother—they are the hosts of the Egyptian initiates, all of them dead, burying one who is dead. She, the earlier Isis, has come down to earth and her forces can now be experienced in the earth itself. The son is restored to the mother; it now rests with him to unite fully with her. Through the kind of initiation depicted in this raising, Christ has laid in the young man of Nain a seed which can only blossom in his next incarnation. The youth of Nain becomes a great prophet, a mighty teacher of religion.

In the third century AD Mani or Manes, the founder of Manicheism, appeared in Babylon. The legend has it that Scythianos and Terebinthus or Buddha were his predecessors. After the violent death of Scythianos, Terebinthus takes his books and flees to Babylon. Only one aged widow accepts his teaching. She inherits the books and leaves them to her twelve year old foster son whom she had adopted when he was a slave boy of seven years. This youth—who once again can be called the 'Son of a Widow' appears at the age of 24 as Manes, the founder of Manicheism. His teaching embraced all the wisdom of the ancient religions, the Babylonian-Egyptian star wisdom, the Persian religion and even the ancient Indian religion, and filled them with the Christ Impulse. He worked as a preparer. This soul was previously the young man of Nain and was initiated by Christ for future times when Manicheism will have reached its full development and will come to light for the salvation of the ancient people of the East. In his incarnation as Manes this soul worked in preparation for his later mission—for the true union of all religions.

For this to be possible this soul had to be born again as one who stands in a *special relationship* to the Christ Impulse. All the ancient and new wisdom of Manes had to come down again. As the 'pure fool' he had to confront the external knowledge of the world and the working of the Christ Impulse in the depths of his own soul. He is born again as Parsifal, the son of Herzeleide, the tragic figure whose husband Gamuret had forsaken her. As the 'Son of the Widow' he too abandons his mother and goes out into the world. After many wanderings he comes to be chosen as the Guardian of the Holy Grail. The Parsifal legend tells us how he goes to the East and finds his brothers in the members of the dark race. To them also will one day come the blessings of the Holy Grail. Thus in his life as Parsifal he prepares to become, later on, a new teacher of Christianity whose mission it will be to permeate Christianity more and more deeply with the teachings of karma and reincarnation—when the time is ripe for this.

Hiram and Lazarus

The second post-Atlantean epoch is that of Zarathustra. Christ Jesus could not therefore awaken Zarathustra as the appointed representative of the second epoch. But another individuality was incarnated on earth at that time; one whose evolution and all-important mission for humanity are in a remarkable way parallel with those of Zarathustra. This individuality was Lazarus, the reborn Hiram, the Syrian master builder, the greatest of the sons of Cain, who had also worked his mission of the earth out of the human ego, as Zarathustra had done in Ancient Persia. Lazarus is 'sick' and 'dies' and is laid in the grave. Jesus speaks to His disciples of Lazarus' death ('He sleepeth'). Then Thomas, who is called 'twin', says to the disciples 'Let us also go, that we may die with him' (John 11:16). In the awakening of Lazarus that is to take place, the souls belonging to the second post-Atlantean epoch are represented by Thomas the 'twin'. The seed of culture that lived in the ancient Persian epoch has not died—therefore it is not a matter of awakening one *who is dead* but of the *initiation of one who is alive*. That is the great difference in the story between this awakening and the other two. The awakening of Lazarus stands in the centre of St John's Gospel. In the first part it is the testimony of John the Baptist that the Christ Being will appear in the flesh. In the second part it is the testimony of the disciple 'whom Jesus loved'—the awakened Lazarus. One is the Old John, the other the New John. But through the Christ Being the ancient form of initiation had to be replaced by the new one. For this however a transition was needed from olden times to new times. Thus Christ chose Lazarus, who is initiated in the old way but into Christian esotericism. This could only be performed by Christ who indicated that 'this sickness is not unto death, but for the glory of God, that the Son of God might be glorified thereby' (John 11:4). Therefore the Christ speaks the words: 'I am the resurrection and the life: he that believeth in me, though he were dead, yet shall he live.' (John 11:25) Christ comes to the grave wherein Lazarus, supposedly dead, has been laid, and before all the people He utters the sacramental words: 'Lazarus, come forth.' Christ speaks the words which indicate that from now onwards this initiate will begin to work: 'Loose him, and let him go.' He is not a youth like the man of Nain; he is a grown man in full possession of his spiritual forces. And the awakened Lazarus becomes the writer of the John Gospel. He is the one who stands under the cross to whom Christ speaks the words 'Behold thy Mother', meaning the Sophia-Maria. This is evidence that the ego of Zarathustra, who was the Solomon child, was actually born as the son of this mother. With this power within him he can work, even before the sixth post-Atlantean epoch. In the fifth epoch he is already preparing the sixth that will show the deepest understanding for the Christ Impulse and the Gospel of St John.

Ancient India and the daughter of Jairus

The cultural epoch of Ancient India is the oldest and most spiritual one. Its descendants lived at the time of Christ Jesus, as well as in our own time, although the culture has now become materialistic. This is the epoch whose resurrection will be the last of all; the epoch that must wait longest. This resurrection is narrated in a mysterious way in the story of the awakening of the twelve year old daughter of Jairus and in the healing of the woman who for twelve years had suffered from an issue of blood (Mark 6:22-43). The girl is near death; Christ is to heal her. But the woman, whose illness began at the birth of the girl, is also alive. The blood and life is streaming away from her. She represents what has become of the culture of Ancient India, which had once blossomed forth with such wonderful spirituality. The woman is karmically bound to the girl who is twelve years old—that means that the etheric body is near to completion. The seed that had been laid in the etheric body during the period of Ancient India was to be awakened and preserved for the last, seventh epoch. But this awakening can only take place if the woman is healed. She comes from 'behind', touches the hem of Christ's garment and is healed because 'thy faith hath made thee whole' (Mark 5:34). She is healed because within her, by her own free will, she has faith in the Spirit who is incarnate in flesh upon the earth. A great host is around the twelve year old dead girl, weeping and wailing. They belong to the first epoch and are mourning for that spirit which is past. The mysteries enacted in these awakenings were meant to remain for long ages, unknown and hidden.

In these three awakenings we recognise the Three Kings who brought gold from Persia, frankincense from India, and myrrh from Egypt-Chaldea.

7
A Miracle for Our Time

Do we still have miracles in our time? Some would reluctantly agree and many more would definitely say 'yes'.

We have so many religious sects and communities today. In the times when Rudolf Steiner spoke about the miracles[18] of Christ Jesus, however, people had lost their belief in miracles because they had lost the ability to marvel, to wonder, to be amazed. The earlier years of this century were still deeply involved in the last remnants of the materialistic world conception of the late nineteenth century, whereas today there are once again so many religious disciples to be found and the Islamic faith spreads rapidly, as do other religions mainly of the East. There are also many faith healers, nature cure-centres and so on, that one frequently hears references to 'miracles', and not only in a manner of speech.

Now let us ask: 'What is a miracle?' A definition often heard claims that a miracle is an unexpected event that is ultimately inexplicable, but works in a certain way in which one has to believe. This would be the *definition* in our time and for our time, but not the *description* of the working of miracles. This is partly due to the form of education we receive today which prevents our children from experiencing wonder and amazement. In the world of mechanics and silicon chips nothing is miraculous any more; nothing to make one stand and stare in wonder. There is only sensation and because young people today have lost the feeling for the miraculous they soon become bored with the sensational.

That is the significant difference between when we speak of a miracle today and when one spoke of it in the times of Jesus. People today more or less have confidence in the miraculous without exactly *knowing* what it is and how it works. In the times of Christ one knew that a miracle was an *act of healing*. That describes a miracle without defining it and those on whom Christ performed the act of healing were usually those whose sickness not only affected the body but also the soul or mind and spirit. The force which prevents man from true wonder or amazement is the total lack of reverence towards anything spiritual or divine. Goethe, in his educational principle in *Wilhelm Meister**, speaks of three reverences man owes to his environment: the reverence for what is below us, the reverence for what is about us and the reverence for what is above us. The sensations which surround us every day do not evoke reverence and the sensational does not awaken in man any feelings of the wonderful or the miraculous. Only in spiritual science can we still feel the wonder, the miraculous, which calls for reverence.

If we are not only to believe in miracles but also *understand* them, we must consider the change which human consciousness has undergone in the course of our whole evolution. The consciousness of the world and with it the consciousness of the self (self-consciousness) was a faculty which man had to acquire by degrees; but it was purchased at the cost of his old clairvoyance.[19] In the future man will regain it again, although then it will be united with self-consciousness. So we have to accept that in the course of evolution everything changes.

Nothing remains the same. Not even the relationship of one man to another was as it is now. The influence of one soul upon another was much stronger in ancient times than it is now. Through that influence from soul to soul those signs or miracles could still happen and could be experienced. Feelings were very different in former times and had a more intimate character but gradually have grown weaker. But they will regain their former strength when the Christ Impulse has entered every human heart. When love was exercised in those times it carried with it something like a healing force flowing as a balm from one soul into another. So that all miracles performed by Christ, or a soul endowed with the Christ spirit, were acts and processes of healing.

Now we must ask what is healing in connection with the

* Johann Wolfgang von Goethe, *Wilhelm Meister* (Volumes I to VI) (London, John Calder, 1980)

sensation of pain. Today we resort to 'pain killers' and so deprive ourselves of the understanding of the nature and sensation of pain. But pain is an indicator that something in an organism is disturbed and we call this disturbance rightly sickness, and sickness must be healed.

Rudolf Steiner explained it in the following way; suppose your favourite occupation or hobby is watering flowers every day. One morning the watering can has disappeared, either lost or stolen. You are sad, you feel deprived or as we would say, it is sickening. But this is no physical pain. It lies more in the deprivation of your favourite occupation. You cannot perform a certain action because the instrument for it is not there. What here causes pain, first moral pain through the deprivation, turns into physical pain in this way: we have a finger in its natural perfect form. If I cut my finger then it is only the physical form of the finger (the etheric and astral finger I cannot cut) so it happens that the ether and astral finger cannot intervene in the way that they are used to with a healthy uncut finger and my activity is disturbed, just as it was before when I could not find my watering can. This disturbance of an activity we feel as pain and therefore have to exercise a greater activity in the etheric and astral body to bring about *healing*. An increased effort is needed, a heightened activity is needed, to bring about healing. This stronger activity, this effort to get well, is needed and this is actually the cause that brings the healing of the organism about. That which calls for a greater activity of the spiritual members of man is *truly healing* and this greater effort of the spiritual part of man is necessary to bring order again into the organism which has come into disorder.

The great poet Novalis said that sickness in man is actually a musical problem because it creates a dissonance where normally there would be order and harmony.

We can learn from this contemplation how important this heightened activity is for real healing, even if a sickness cannot be healed. Then it is karma, but the increased spiritual effort remains and strengthens the weakness of the body for a future life on earth. What matters is that we contribute as much as possible to a real healing, whether this healing comes about or not.

Now that we know what healing in reality is, we have to get acquainted with the reality of sickness or illness. We follow here the example of Rudolf Steiner, who frequently placed the healer or physician *before* the sickness (for example in evolution the ancient Sun before the split of the ancient Moon.[20] So it seems to be also an evolutionary principle).

In the previous example of the cut finger we recognised sickness as the state of an organ in separation from the whole to which it originally belonged. Therefore sickness can be compared with a gaping wound, with healing only occurring if the two separated parts become *whole* again; the other meaning of whole being healthy, being one again.

The world, which in the course of evolution separated more and more, has today become a yawning abyss. The power to close the abyss, to heal the breach between cosmos and earth needs more and more effort for the process of healing. The theme of the gaping wound occurs throughout the whole legend of the Holy Grail. Through a moral defect the King Amfortas suffers from a wound which can only be healed through the pure untainted hero who finds the miraculous spear which caused the wound. The immaculate hero is Parsifal, who has not yet forgotten how to wonder and be amazed. There is a very subtle relationship between wonder and wound, clearer in the German (*wunder* and *wunde*) and beautifully united by Richard Wagner, expressed in the designation: '*O wunden—wundervoller speer*'. The healing of the wound is the uniting of what has been separated. This spear, which is the one which on Golgotha was thrust into the side of Him who was crucified, opened the flow of Christ's blood which healed the earth and the whole of mankind.

In seven steps of healing St John unfolds before us the Seven Signs or miracles culminating in the raising of Lazarus. These are the seven miracles:

1. The marriage in Cana, Galilee
2. The healing of the nobleman's son
3. The healing at the pool of Bethesda
4. The feeding of the five thousand
5. Christ walking on the sea
6. The healing of the man born blind
7. The raising of Lazarus

Now after a long journey of discovery we have come nearer to the understanding of a miracle and also how to describe it instead of

defining it. It is the third of the miracles: the healing of the man
(who had an infirmity for 38 years) at the pool of Bethesda (St
John 5:2-15).

Here again we must read significant words which throw the
most light on the matter. It is the passage which reads: 'Jesus saith
unto him, Rise, take up thy bed, and walk.' The impotent man had
previously said: 'Sir, I have no man when the water is troubled to
put me into the pool.' What we said at the beginning comes now
into bearing when Christ in effect says: make the effort yourself,
move, if you want to be cured, rise up, change your position (the
bed in which we lie stands here for destiny, irrelevant to whether
it is a mattress or a four poster), do not lie down inactively and
expect to be healed, but rise and walk. Christ is pointing here to
a specific process of healing. And the further sequence: 'Behold,
thou art made whole: sin no more, lest a worse thing comes unto
thee.'

As before we find that what was said about sickness is again
connected with morality. Sin has the same meaning as sickness,
the separation of the whole, the human soul from the spiritual
world. Healing is an act of reuniting the two separates; the closing
of the wound through the wonder. We need not enquire whether
the sin he had committed was in his present or in his former life.
We are concerned with the fact that Christ poured into his soul
the power to do something which moved the depth of his moral
and soul nature. Here we have an infirmity which Christ Himself
said is connected with the sin of the infirm man. At that moment
Christ can pierce to the man's very soul. His power works into the
soul of the infirm man.

This event was performed on a sabbath day. This was for the
Old Testament believers quite unusual. They could not take it as
a matter of course that the infirm man was healed on a Sabbath;
that he could suddenly use his limbs and that it is lawful to carry
one's bed. In Christ himself dwells the thought: If the Sabbath is
truly sanctified by God the souls of men must be especially
fortified by the power of God on that day. It is not the stagnant
waters of that pool which have the life giving power, but the living
water stirred by the Angel whose element it is that can give the
impotent man that help he needs to heal his sickness and his sins.
The water cleanses man of his iniquities in the past; it bestows in
the baptism the whole reunification of cosmos and earth—our

primeval picture being the baptism in Jordan where the Christ spirit penetrates the whole body of Jesus of Nazareth, right into his very bones.

This is the message of the miracle for our time, the third of the signs; that whereas we are sick and had hitherto lacked the strength to overcome the consequences of our sins we know now how to get this strength through our own endeavour with the power of Christ.

And now to end this contemplation in an appropriate manner let me say:

1. 'Rise' your *thinking* from sluggish inactivity through great effort to the living water which the Angel stirs.
2. 'Take your destiny upon you' to purify your *soul* from past sins—to heal your body from these consequences and;
3. 'Walk': use your limbs as an upright man who knows his goal.

These are the three *new* gifts which come to us from this third sign or miracle for the right progress into the future, a New Epiphany.

8
The Healing of the Man Born Blind

The 'healing of the man born blind' is the sixth miracle in the seven steps of healing which St John unfolds before us as the Seven Signs or miracles,[21] culminating in the 'raising of Lazarus'. It refers to the inmost recesses of the human soul, which bears a germ of the divine. It is something godlike in man and upon this the Christ works. It requires a very deep understanding to follow the further step of the healing of the blindness through the power of the Christ, which increases with each miracle he performs. Working upon the divine germ in the blind man, we find also a more profound understanding for the question of the disciples, 'Master, who did sin, this man, or his parents?' and the answer of the Christ: 'Neither hath this man sinned, nor his parents: but that the works of God should be made manifest in him.' (St John 9:2-3)

This sixth miracle Rudolf Steiner calls the greatest and most significant of all, for here Christ works with the divine principle in man indicated by the words, 'that the works of God should be made manifest in him' (usually wrongly interpreted). The divine principle in man is different from his personality living here on earth between birth and death and is also different from that which man inherits from his parents. This divine spark, this individuality of the human being, is that which passes from incarnation to incarnation through repeated lives on earth. It comes from a former life on earth, from an earlier incarnation. Thus neither his parents have sinned nor has his personality, his 'I'; but it was in a former life that he laid down the cause of his blindness in his present life. He became blind in order that the works of the God, proceeding from a former life, should reveal themselves in him in his blindness. *Karma*, the law of cause and effect, is here most clearly indicated by the Christ. To awaken the *self-healing* forces in man the influence of the Christ must work, not upon the *transitory 'Ego'*,[22] living between birth and death, but must pierce deeper into the Ego that passes from life to life. Thus man receives through the divine in him the strength to heal himself from within his being.

What is the divine being in man? To find the answer we have to look at the chapter before the healing of the blind man when Christ says, 'I am the light of the world'. The power of the 'I am' Christ refers to as Himself, and it is now active on earth as the power of healing the blindness of the world through the 'I am'.[23] The benighted soul, the darkness of the spirit, turns despairingly to the Light which now fills and radiates the earth.

How did this mysterious act of healing come about? How is it described in the Gospel of St John? 'He spat on the ground, and made clay of the spittle, and anointed the eyes of the blind man with the clay. And said unto him, Go, wash in the pool of Siloam. He went his way therefore, and washed, and came seeing.'

What we see demonstrated here is that the healing force of the Christ appears now in its full power. The power is in the Body of the Christ which is the Earth; also confirmed in the words: 'He who eats My Bread treads me underfoot.'[24] Again an 'I am' word: 'I am the bread of life'. (Seven 'I am' words between Bread and Wine.)

Now let us take the description of the miracle further and take it literally. Imagine we have before us two persons; one is a corpse, the other one alive. They are placed side by side. When we have a *living, waking* human being before us, we know that a soul and a spirit dwell within him. But as far as his consciousness is concerned the light of the spiritual world is extinguished in him. His soul and spirit live in darkness; blind to the light of the spirit-world. Man is not aware of it while he lives.

And now for the other example. We have a corpse before us. We have the feeling that the spirit and the soul which once belonged to it are passing over into the spiritual worlds where the light of those worlds is flashing up within them. Thus the corpse becomes a symbol of what is taking place in the spiritual world. Its light becomes visible in the corpse. So that when a man is reborn on earth the light of the spiritual world *dies* for him and he *awakens* for the physical world. We, all of us, are born blind for the spirit worlds and their working in the earth.

On the other hand, at the moment of decomposition, or of the burning of the physical body, when parts disintegrate and dissolve, the opposite becomes manifest; namely, the light of the spiritual world and an awakening of the spiritual consciousness occurs. *Physical decay is spiritual birth.*

How does this apply to the healing of the man born blind?

> 'And as Jesus passed by, he saw a man which was blind from his birth. And the disciples asked him, saying, Master, who did sin, this man, or his parents, that he was born blind? Jesus answered, Neither hath this man sinned, nor his parents: but that the works of God should be made manifest in him. I must work the works of him that sent me, while it is day: the night cometh, when no man can work. As long as I am in the world, I am the light of the world. When he had thus spoken, he spat on the ground, and made clay of the spittle, and he anointed the eyes of the blind man with the clay, and said unto him, Go, wash in the pool of Siloam ... He went his way therefore, and washed, and came seeing. The neighbours therefore, and they which before had seen him that he was blind, said, Is not this he that sat and begged? ... he said: I am *he*. Therefore said they unto him, How were thine eyes opened? He answered and said, A man that is called Jesus made clay, and anointed mine eyes, and said unto me, Go to the pool of Siloam, and wash; and I went and washed, and I received sight. Then said they unto him, Where is he? He said, I know not. They brought to the Pharisees him that aforetime was blind. And it was the Sabbath day when Jesus made the clay, and opened his eyes. Then again the Pharisees asked him how he had received his sight ... [he told them the same story] ... Therefore said some of the Pharisees, This man is not of God, because he keepeth not the Sabbath day' (John 9:1-16).[25]

The Jews then called the parents and asked them if this was their son who was born blind and how he could now see. And the parents replied that this was their son who was born blind. 'He is of age; ask him: he shall speak for himself. These *words* spake his parents, because they feared the Jews.'

Now let us depict the whole event and observe its stages. Standing there is the blind man. Christ takes some earth, insalivates it, and lays it upon the blind man's eyes. He lays His Body, the earth permeated with His Spirit, upon the blind man. In this description the writer of the Gospel indicates the mystery which he himself very well understands. This sign—one of the greatest performed by Christ—was given in order that we may better understand the nature of such a sign. There are in the world great and mighty mysteries which mankind is *not yet entitled to know*. Human beings of today, even though they may be sufficiently developed, are *not yet strong enough* to go through great mysteries. Our present humanity is too deeply immersed in matter and is not yet capable of going right through the Mysteries and into the final physical consequences of this.

Let us now take the case of a certain training in which one schools oneself to breathe in putrified air which arises out of the decomposition of a human corpse, with the intention of taking that spirit-light and the spiritual processes which we have just described.[26] (Students of forensic medicines simply faint when smelling a decomposed corpse.)

Breathing in putrid air belongs to a schooling which gradually gives strength to the spittle, when mixed with ordinary earth, to become a *healing* substance; which the Christ rubbed upon the eyes of the blind man. The mystery by which a person inhales death, by which he acquires the power to heal, is also described in Dostoevsky's *Brothers Karamazov** in the scene when Alyosha keeps watch over the dead body of his great teacher, the Staretz Sossima, and imbues him with powers to heal mankind. It is the true mystery to which the writer of the Gospel refers when describing such a 'sign' as 'the healing of the blind'. The healing of the man born blind is literally true. There was such a person who was thoroughly initiated into the mysteries about which we must try to acquire *understanding*. One day, when all prejudices are eliminated, it will become possible to speak of such real mysteries as the salivation of the earth's soil for healing purposes, and to say that such an incident has a literal significance.

Knowing now these facts, let us try to comprehend the ideas that occupy us today, namely that Christ is the *Spirit of the earth*,

* Fyodor Dostoevsky, *Brothers Karamazov* (London, Pengiun, 1989)

and that the earth is His Body. He gives up something of Himself (the spittle, unified with the earth) in order to heal the blind man.

But apart from what we have said today, let us hear what Christ Himself has said: 'The most profound mystery of My Being is the 'I am' and the true and eternal might must flow into human beings. It dwells within the Earth Spirit.'[27] Christ wishes to bestow the true Ego upon every human soul. He will awaken the God in it and gradually kindle the Spirit of the Lord in everyone. That signifies that the Christ Being brings to expression, in the highest sense, the idea of karma, the karmic law, which works itself out on earth, through our life on earth.

Furthermore, to understand this sign in its true reality, so that the question of the disciples cannot be misunderstood, we have to realise that Christ works the individual karma of the blind man into the great karma of the Earth. Our individual karma, so Rudolf Steiner says, is constantly intersected by the greater karma of the Earth itself, the karma of humanity, and the still greater karma of the Cosmos or the Universe because even the Gods have, to a certain extent, a 'karma'.

But the greater karma of the Earth itself has now Christ as its Lord. He became the Judge replacing Moses. Therefore the karmic judgement lies with the Christ. We might interpret the question of the disciples as a judgement: who has *sinned* that as a consequence the man is born blind?

They could have asked simply: 'Why is this man blind?' Therefore Christ admonishes the disciples not to judge because if one man judges another, the one is always placing the other under the compulsion of his own self. Therefore if a person really believes in Christ as the divine 'I am' he will not judge. He will know that Karma is the great adjuster. The example which the Christ here sets before his disciples is his admonition. In effect what Christ is saying is: 'Whether what you maintain has been done by him or not makes no difference. The *I am* must be respected; it must be left to karma, to the great law of the Christ Spirit himself.'

Anthroposophy tells us that the Christ is now the Lord of karma, so we come to realise the very deep significance of His Being for the Earth. Therefore we find in this miracle a constant metamorphosis of the words: 'I am the light of the world.' This light is connected with the cosmic 'I' as the true light of the sun, which radiates out of the Six Elohim which have remained with the sun, the Christ Being. We now realise the significance of this sixth miracle.

Let us remember the words of Rudolf Steiner on this subject — thus commemorating His earthly birth as a cosmic event on earth: The 'healing of the man born blind' is not a magic miracle, but a deed of enlightenment, of transfiguration, or awakening. It is therefore an act of initiation.

9
The Mission of Joan of Arc in Relation to St Paul

Joan of Arc

Between the idealistic conception of Schiller's *The Maid of Orlean* and the realistic representation of Bernard Shaw's *Joan of Arc* stands Rudolf Steiner's description of Joan of Arc as the 'first Christian sibyl'.

It is certainly not easy to unravel the riddles of visions, prophesies, imaginations and spiritual revelations in our time. They appear and proliferate like mushrooms. But some light can be thrown on them. Some understanding is gained through Rudolf Steiner's description of these very remarkable manifestations of spiritual life: the sibyls. The sibyls were indeed a remarkable phenomenon with a prophetic character entirely of their own. Their prophesies show that they arose from strange, subconscious regions of human nature and soul life. Far removed from anything like orderly thought, the utterances of the sibyls poured out visions like a spiritual fanatic who wants to force upon people what he has to say. They did not wait to be questioned (like the ancient Oracles) but poured out their utterances with overbearing force.

Historically we hear of the most varied kinds of sibyls throughout the Greco-Roman epoch, with their psychic products emanating from the chaos of their souls, driven by elemental spirits of fire, air, water and earth. Sometimes they shedded true illuminations on the future; but more often they announced things which were falsified and had to be corrected afterwards, to give the impression that their prophesy had been fulfilled.

We see these sibyls accompanying the fourth cultural epoch like a shadow of wisdom, spreading through Greece and Italy until we come to the Mystery of Golgotha. How much importance was attached to their sayings is shown by the so called 'Sibylline

Books', to which one turned for guidance. And again we see how in connection with the sibylline sayings great intelligence is chaotically mixed up with arrogant humbug. Even today, when we hear a requiem mass, we see sibylism has gained a foothold in Christian liturgy. Who would not be deeply shaken by the dramatic entry in Mozart's *Requiem: 'Dies irae, dies illae, solve saeclum in favilla, teste David cum Sibylla'* (Day of wrath, O day which leads this world-age into destruction, according to the testimony of David and the Sybil). Incidentally the *Dies irae* prevails as a sinister reckoning throughout the last movement of Berlioz's *Fantastic symphony.*

In the great painting in the Sistine Chapel Michelangelo depicts in a grand manner the contrast between the sibyls and the prophets. The prophets are deeply reflective men, for the most part absorbed in books, quietly taking in, in a well-ordered state of mind, whatever it is they are studying. In the countenance of these prophets we encounter the calmness of their souls. They are all absorbed in super-earthly things; their souls are at rest in the spiritual.

In the gestures and movements of the sibyls we see how they are connected with everything that comes to man from the elemental secrets of the earth. Here is human passion, kindling out of the unconscious soul forces, the message that is to be instilled with all the power of prophecy into mankind. The prophets are devoted in their souls to the primal eternity of the spirit; the sibyls are carried away by the earthly in so far as it reveals the soul-spiritual.

And so two quite different developments can be traced. On the one hand there is the world of concepts, a world of ideas which could be called the purest form of the spiritual world. The second element which persisted from older times is an atavistic element, an heirloom, and it persisted most plainly in the prophesies of the sibyls.

Man could have fallen under the spell of elemental spirits. Their teachers would have been of the sibylline kind and their strong force would have persisted right up to the present day, and indeed up to the very end of Earth's days.

This did not happen. That the Sibylline forces gradually declined was due to the fact that Christ, through the Mystery of Golgotha, infused the aura of the earth with His Being. He destroyed the Sibylline force in the souls of men, and with this transformed Sibylline force *Joan of Arc* was born.

In the cycle of the year the most intimate connection with the spiritual worlds happens from about 24 December to 6 January. During this period the Christ Impulse is not yet hindered by the influences of the earth, so that this impulse can penetrate right into the soul. This was the most favourable time for the birth of the Maid of Orleans. Before she drew her first breath she was still passing through the Thirteen Holy Nights in her mother's womb. She was born on 6 January 1412. Through this marvellous birth she went through an unconscious initiation up to the time of Epiphany. The Christ Impulse could flow into the deeds of the people of that time, but this was not accomplished by those who were most advanced at the time. It was, however, fulfilled by the poor shepherd-maiden of Orleans.

The age demanded that the impulse which the Maid of Orleans was to work from should come from the gentlest and most subtle forces of the human soul. Rudolf Steiner presents this to us by quoting from a letter which the counsellor and chamberlain Percival, Duke of Orleans, writes to the Duke of Milan: 'The girl is of appealing beauty and manly bearing; she speaks little and shows remarkable sagacity. When she speaks she has a pleasing delicately feminine voice. She endures unheard of toil and is so assiduous in fulfilling her tasks that she remains uninterrupted for six days and nights in full armour' (written at Biteromis, 21 June 1429). Early in life she had visions and through these she was in direct contact with the spiritual world. The Christ Being worked through the Maid of Orleans by means of His Michael Spirit, and not through what men understood of Him.

Joan of Arc accomplished the unique deed, which ultimately was to change the map of Europe and furthered the progress of the Christ Impulse on earth. Her courageous *deed* was the living prophecy of the future of Europe through the Christ Impulse, and in this sense Rudolf Steiner calls her 'the first sibyl, deeply imbued with the Christ Impulse'. Under her influence and her inspiration the Christ Impulse fully permeated, although invisibly, the history of Europe, beginning in the autumn of 1428.

But something else had to happen if her mission was to be fully successful. France needed a crowned King to prove to the English that they had no right to France. In the same letter by the Duke of

Orleans, who called himself Percival, he writes: 'Still more wonderful things are happening and have happened. The Maid has already gone to the neighbourhood of the city of Rheims in Champagne whither the King has hastily set off for his anointing (*huile sacre*) to be crowned under God's protection.'

French chronicles report that the Holy Phial, with the oil preserved intact in the tomb of St Remi, had been taken by the English. They boasted that they had taken possession of the only true Holy Oil. The Virgin Mother herself had given it to Thomas of Canterbury when he took refuge in France. Joan of Arc proved that fact not to be true. She had preserved and already brought the Holy Oil to the Archbishop for the anointing. Thus Charles VII had become King of France by Divine Right and Joan was the first to kneel before him.[28]

St Paul

There is another person of whom Rudolf Steiner says almost exactly the same thing as of Joan of Arc, and this person is St Paul. St Paul stands in the midst of a world where something is going on beyond the reach of his words. But if one wants to grasp what lives there between the words spiritually, there is much more than one gets from simply reading the text. One feels what spiritually lived in Paul, which is akin to the sibyls; but with him—like Joan of Arc—it proceeds from a good element of the earth radiating in the aura of the earth, very different to that of the sibyls. In the case of Paul it emerged from his vision at Damascus and the Etheric Christ who now lives in the aura of the good element of the earth. What Paul created out of the good elemental nature of the earth was active in a distinctive region of the earth.

Paul is great throughout the world where the Olive tree is cultivated. The region where the Olive tree flourishes is different from the regions where the Oak or the Ash flourish. In the world of the olive tree the rustle and movement, the whisper and gesture, are not the same as in the world of the Oak or the Ash or the Yew. Paul carries his message just as far as the domain of the Olive tree extends. The world of Paul is the world of the Olive tree. In that geographical realm of the Olive tree the elemental forces could inspire him. Paul describes his work in this realm in words newly minted out of the elemental depths of his soul: [paraphrased version follows of Romans 11:13-24]

'But I have something to say to you Gentiles. I am
missionary to the Gentiles and as such give all honour to
the ministry. I speak to you of the life which emanates from
the dead. If the root of the olive tree is consecrated so are
the branches. But some of the branches have been lopped
off, and you, wild olive tree have been grafted in among
them and have come to share the same root and sap as the
olive tree. Do not make yourself superior to the branches.
Remember: it is not you who sustains the root: the root
sustains you. For if you were cut from your native wild
olive and grafted into the cultivated one how much more
readily would you shed the wild olive for the cultivated
one.'

These are St Paul's superb pictures of what reigns in the domain
of the Olive tree.

We have now reached the point where we can understand the
difference between the development of people and the continu-
ous development of the single human individuality. Joan of Arc
changed, through her individual deeds, the whole future history
of Europe, beginning with the anointing of the dauphin and thus
giving a new king to France.

Paul, through his individual experience of the Risen Christ,
could work for the cultivating forces of the Olive tree against the
wild ones (the taming of the sibylline forces) among the Gentiles.

I consider it more than sheer coincidence, especially in a
lecture cycle, when Rudolf Steiner weaves his words around Joan
of Arc and St Paul. Their common mission, as I see it, was the
taming and suppressing of the wild, chaotic sibylline forces
through the Christ Impulse. What they achieved is, in a realistic
spiritual way, connected with the oil of a plant which, from a wild
state through grafting turns into a cultivated one. This was also
instrumental in the fulfillment of Joan of Arc's mission to see to
the anointing of the French King, which changed the whole
future of Europe.

An old legend tells us that the dying Adam asked his son Seth to
bring him the 'oil of mercy' from Paradise, so that he could die in
peace. The subsiding of the flood was announced to Noah by a
dove bringing an olive branch to indicate God's peace with man.
We hear that Samuel anointed Saul as King with the holy oil

without crowning him. Last but not least there were the wise virgins who preserved their sacred oil that their own lamps may lighten up the path of the Risen Christ.

The task I set myself in this lecture was to confront this sacred or cultivated oil, the 'oil of mercy' with the crude oil of the earth which is today the scourge of our world and which Paul would have called the 'wild' one. This so called 'energy problem' stops the wheels of industrial life and strangles all movements between people through greed. To confront the sacred 'oil of mercy' with that exploited by greed, to place these two side by side was the aim I set myself. To think of a grafting of the 'spiritually cultivated' oil upon the wild one is a goal of the future in so far as we continue to work on and with the Christ Impulse, like our two friends Joan of Arc and St Paul did. What remains now is to give the reason why we have chosen the final scene of Schiller's *Maid of Orleans*. It conveys in a very intimate way the union of the Shepherdess with the King in her devotion to him. We might consider it as her last mission to unite the stream represented by the Shepherds, who herald the future Christ Impulse, with that of the Kings who represent a glorious past.

Rudolf Steiner made this remark about Schiller's *Maid of Orleans*: 'It is natural to the German intellectual life, since the great work of Schiller, to comprehend the Maid of Orleans from the supersensible side; whereas in Anatole France we have a man who comprehends Joan of Arc from the most intellectual and materialistic standpoint of the present day. But the essential thing is that we possess this work of Schiller which undertook, from the depth of spiritual life, to picture the glorious resurrection of this figure of whom Schiller writes: "The world loves to blacken the radiant, and to drag the sublime into dust."'*

* Rudolf Steiner, *Occult History* (London, Rudolf Steiner Press, 1982)

10
The Spiritual Background to St Francis of Assisi

Whoever wishes to speak of Francis should ask for a warm heart and true simplicity, without which the task is impossible. He was the most extraordinary man of his age.

Francis was the son of a rich cloth-merchant Pietro Bernardone. He was born in 1182 or 83 and his coming was like the coming of a fresh spring breeze to a tired world. It was said that his mother, full of apprehension of a difficult birth, asked to be taken down to the stable, where almost at once she gave birth to a very healthy boy. Thus even at his birth Francis resembles Jesus, for he also began his earthly life in a stable.

A man's earthly life begins at his birth, but the spiritual life that leads to eternity begins at his baptism. The son of Pietro Bernardone was on his mother's instructions—prompted by a dream—named John, after the Baptist. But when his Father came back from France after a very successful business deal, he insisted that his son should be called Francis as a perpetual reminder of the land where he was so successful and which he loved so well.

What sort of a person was Francis of Assisi as a youth? He was one who conducted himself like a descendent of the old German knights, and this need not appear remarkable when we consider how people intermingled after the immigration from the North. Brave, warlike, filled with the ideal of winning honour and fame with the weapons of war; it was this which existed as a heritage, as a racial characteristic in the personality of Francis of Assisi. On the occasion of a quarrel between Assisi and Perugia he and his comrades were taken prisoners. He not only bore his captivity patiently and in a knightly way, but he encouraged all the others to do the same until a year later when they were able to return home. After his return to Assisi Francis had a kind of dialogue with a spirit-being which said: 'Not in external service have you to seek your knighthood. You are destined to transform all the forces at your disposal into powers of the soul, into weapons forged for your use. All the weapons you saw in the palace signify the spiritual weapons of mercy, compassion and love.'

Francis fell for some time into a severe illness and after his recovery the young knight, who in his boldest dreams had only longed to become a great warrior, was transformed into a man who now most earnestly sought all the impulses of mercy, compassion and love. All the shields he so often used in his skirmishes signified to him a reasoning power by which to defend himself. He now resolved to fulfil literally the counsels of the Gospels, and he took a vow to live in complete poverty and never to refuse a beggar an alm. He sold all his precious clothes to give money to the poor and to help the monks to restore their abbeys. All the forces he had thought of using in the services of the physical world were transformed into *moral impulses.*[29]

Pietro Bernardone, his father, cited him before the magistrate in order to compel him to renounce his inheritance. Francis abandoned all and declared that henceforth he had but one father only, the one 'which is in Heaven'. Here we see how a *moral impulse* evolves in a single personality.

This tremendous turning point in Francis' life occurred in his twenty-sixth year in 1208. In 1212 he finally settled the simple constitution of his order. He rejected all forms of property for his order and its members. Even the gowns they wore were not their property, nor the cord which girded their loins. In these actions were concentrated all the moral intentions which evolved out of the heroism of his youth. These concentrated moral impulses had transformed his former bravery into soul forces of the highest moral order. Through them he felt an inner personal relationship to the Cross and the Christ. He led the life of an ascetic in utter poverty and it is said that he received the five stigmata of the Christ on Monte La Verna in the year 1224. He wrote about each one of them and explained their different meanings.

Rudolf Steiner goes further and admonishes us to try and realise that these moral forces are a reality, as real as the air we breathe and without which we cannot live. It is a reality which flooded the whole being of Francis of Assisi and streamed from him into all the hearts to which he dedicated himself. The moral forces streamed and intermingled with the whole mature life of Europe and thus worked in the world of external reality. Rudolf Steiner also asks us to reflect upon the healing effect of such moral forces as were exercised by Francis of Assisi. He was a mystic of a special kind and in this context Rudolf Steiner unfolds before us three kinds of mystics as they appear in the history of mankind. 'Every mystic has three soul experiences. His *consciousness* with self-consciousness, his *heart* and his *brain*.'*

Let us imagine that a mystic feels called upon to break down his self-consciousness for the sake of divine consciousness. He wishes to get beyond the former. He will still have left the use of his heart and his brain. He can have these two experiences while consciousness is extinguished. To find mystics of this first category we have to go rather far back in history. We may find them among those who, after the founding of Christianity, endeavoured to rise to the *divine self* with the help of the philosophy of Plato. The Neoplatonists include Iamblichus and Plotinus. In this class too belongs Scotus Erigena and also Master Eckhart, in whom his brain experiences outweighed the experiences of his heart.

The second kind of mystic is one who shuts out not his consciousness alone, but in addition also his brain experiences, retaining only the ideas and conceptions of the heart. These mystics have no love for anything 'thought-out'. They want to exclude thought altogether as well as consciousness. Only what the heart can achieve: that is all they will allow themselves to use for their development. They base their relationship with the surrounding world on the experience of the heart. But as this kind of mystic is connected with his surroundings through the *heart* alone, he will not find easily accessible the complicated ideas that are acquired on the path of occultism. To receive these one does need to do, at any rate, a little thinking. But in Francis of Assisi the human experience of the heart overshadows all others. He stands in such intimate relation to nature that the sun is his brother, the moon his sister, the water and fire and earth is his mother. Here is a mystic who comes right out beyond ordinary human consciousness, but at the same time retains all these experiences

* Rudolf Steiner, *The Occult Significance of the Bhagavad Gita* (New York, Anthroposophic Press, 1968)

of the soul which are acquired through the heart. He is our mystic, known well by all: Francis of Assisi.

Francis of Assisi is a striking example of a mystic who, at least in one incarnation, rejected all theology and all knowledge of supersensible things. Therefore he was able to live in extraordinary intimacy with the spirits of nature. This was indeed an outstanding feature of his life.

We shall now pass to a third class of mystic, described by Rudolf Steiner. There are mystics who experience ecstasy not through shutting out consciousness nor the heart but through retaining *thoughts* or experiences of the brain. Such men are usually not described as mystics at all. Although in our present day we can't all be like St Francis, yet the universality of the heart in St Francis has a powerful influence upon people, even if the personal element is dulled and suppressed.

But a mystic who suppresses not only his self-consciousness but also his heart experiences and lives in thoughts alone— thoughts bound to the brain—is of little interest to his fellowmen. They will simply not concern themselves with him. The philosopher Hegel is a mystic of the third order, in the true sense of the word. What he gives in his philosophy is expressly intended to exclude every personal point of view. It sets out to be pure contemplation in thought and we may take Hegel as an eminent example of a mystic with *brain* experiences alone. After this slight but important digression we return to the mystic of the heart: Francis of Assisi.

His life shows a remarkable similarity with that of the exalted Gautama Buddha. Both were born rich. The Gautama, who lived in India about 600 BC, was the son of King Sudhodana and lived in a palace; and Francis was the son of a rich cloth merchant. Both gave up their titles and their riches to live in utter poverty: Gautama and his monks travelling barefoot through Benares begging for a bowl of rice; Francis in his infinite compassion living among the lepers. Both in their own special way were chosen to become enlightened leaders of humanity.

To find the reasons for such highly developed individuals Rudolf Steiner points earnestly to the distinction between soul development and race development. The souls reappear in bodies belonging to certain races, the other race bodies die out. When over large areas something disappears, as it were, it does not disappear into nothing, but it dissolves and then exists in a different form. When in ancient times the worst part of the population died out, the whole region became gradually inhabited by demons, representing the products of dissolution and immorality.

But while on the one hand the after-effects of what was immoral and putrified raged, moral forces worked so strongly that they could purify Europe from the substances of old 'disease-demons' which had swept through Europe since the leader Attila, with his hordes of Huns, invaded Europe. This is a striking example of how moral power enters man and how it must be understood as something quite special; a purifying healing force.

Now how had such a soul power come into Francis of Assisi? We can understand a soul such as this if we take the trouble to trace back what was hidden in its depth. We find this hidden depth if we follow the stream of his destiny which leads us to the south-eastern shores of the Black Sea and its Mystery centre and school.

Now we can ask what lies behind the foundation of this Mystery centre?

In the early Christian era, about 400 AD, a great occult conference took place in the spiritual world, concerned with the initiation of Christian Rosenkreuz.[30] He was associated with certain other great individuals, who would lead the future civilisation of humanity on the physical plane, but also those who had a body-free existence in the spiritual world. To begin with pupils in the Mystery school had external teachers. They were instructed in the doctrines and principles which proceeded from great individuals who taught there.

After sufficient preparations the pupils were brought to the deeper forces lying within them, to a deeper wisdom, which made them recognise those teachers who no longer descended to the physical plane. Buddha they recognised as the teacher who taught through his *spirit-body*. He rose in his twenty-ninth year from the rank of Bodhisattva to that of Buddha and no longer appeared on earth in physical incarnation. For the more advanced pupils in this centre of initiation it was possible to receive instructions from one who taught in his etheric body. These pupils were grouped according to their maturity into two unequal divisions and only the more advanced were chosen for the smaller division. This small group of initiates, who also were endowed with deep humility, endeavoured to receive the *Christ Impulse* directly in the manner of St Paul.

Thus Buddhism continued and influenced not only Asiatic life but also those who were imbued with the Christ Impulse throughout Europe. The pupils who had only gained the Buddha-Impulse became teachers of *equality* amongst European men (as opposed to the caste system of India). The other group who had additionally received the *Christ Impulse* worked more through moral powers: moral forces which worked so strongly that they carried healing and purifying capacities.

Among the pupils of the Buddha at that time was one who incarnated again a few centuries later. We are now speaking of a personality who lived in a physical body filled with the Christ Impulse: Francis of Assisi.

If we study the life of Francis of Assisi we note the remarkable course it took. We know that during the first years of his life in a physical body he developed mainly those qualities which originated through external heredity from the European population. These qualities gradually came out as his etheric body developed from the seventh to the fourteenth year, like any other human being. But in his etheric body appeared primarily that quality which, as the Christ Impulse, had worked directly in him in the Mysteries of the Black Sea. From his fourteenth year onwards the Christ power became particularly strong in him—forces which had been in connection with the atmosphere of the earth since the Mystery of Golgotha. For Francis of Assisi was a personality who was permeated by the external power of Christ owing to his having sought for this Christ power in his previous incarnation, in that particular centre of initiation on the Black Sea where it was to be found.

As a pupil of Buddha, Francis of Assisi was, as a most advanced individual, called to a conference in the spiritual world by Christian Rosenkreuz. At that spiritual conference it was resolved that from that time on (beginning of the seventeenth century, about 1604) Buddha would dwell on *Mars* and there unfold his influence and activity. He performed a deed there similar to that of Christ on earth. Christian Rosenkreuz knew that the work of Buddha on Mars would signify for the entire cosmos what his teachings of *Nirvana* and the liberation from earth would mean.

The teaching of *Nirvana* was unsuited to a culture directed primarily to practical life. Buddha's pupil Francis of Assisi was an example of the fact that this teaching produced adepts who were completely remote from the world and its affairs. But the content of this Buddhism was of special importance for the soul *between death and a new birth*.

Christian Rosenkreuz realised that to bring about the certain purification required on Mars, the teachings of Buddha were eminently suitable.

In the seventeenth century Buddha, the Prince of Peace, went to the planet of war and conflict to execute his mission there—where souls were warlike and torn in strife. Through Buddha's deed of redemption of Mars it is possible for us, when passing through the Mars sphere between death and a new birth,[31] to become followers of Francis of Assisi. So since the seventeenth century every human soul is in the Mars sphere for a time as a Buddhist, as Franciscans, as immediate followers of Francis of Assisi. Francis has since made only one brief incarnation on earth, but he died in childhood and did not incarnate again. He is intimately linked with the work of Buddha on Mars and is one of his immediate followers.

Rudolf Steiner placed before our soul a picture of what came about through that important spiritual conference at the end of the sixteenth century, similar to what had happened on earth in the thirteenth century when Christian Rosenkreuz gathered his faithful around him to avert the threatened separation of humanity into two classes (those engaged in outer practical life on earth and the other three categories of mysticism which we met at the beginning of these contemplations, who in one way or the other relinquished the earth conditions). Rosicrucianism united both, hence the great significance of Francis of Assisi, who brought harmony and peace through his transformation of the Mars influences. What distinguished Francis of Assisi most from the human beings of his time was his sublime *faith* in the *goodness* in each human being. Secondly the boundless *love* of man which springs from his *belief*. A third impulse implies the *hope* for each human being that it can find the way back again to the divine-spiritual. These three qualities—faith, belief and hope—were often in his mind during his initiation in the Mysteries of Colchis on the Black Sea. They stand in the centre of his single incarnation as Francis of Assisi, and he carried them forward through the Mars sphere for the moral transformation of humanity towards the divine. This higher order of his endeavours freed him of any lower trace of sentimentality he so often is endowed with.

The great German philosopher Schopenhauer made this very true statement: 'To preach morals is easy, but to give them foundation is difficult.' This we experienced as a fact in Rudolf Steiner's treatment of the life of Francis of Assisi, at that turning point of his life when his knightly heroism became a moral virtue as an individuality imbued in his Ego with the Christ Impulse.

11
The Individuality and Mission
of Raphael

When it was suggested that a festival be arranged to commemo-
rate Raphael's 500th birthday, I decided then and there to support
this valuable initiative.

I intend to speak about Raphael's individuality, rather than the
artistic side. As my talk is partly based on Rudolf Steiner's last
address in 1924* I thought it would be appropriate to choose
Rudolf Steiner's birthday for this occasion.

The transition from painting to poetry shows itself in the
macrocosmic event which the spirit-soul of Raphael underwent
between his death and the birth of Novalis.[32]

'Only an Ego-bearer,' Rudolf Steiner once said, 'can have a
biography.' Such a view widens the concept of biography from the
graphic representation of man's life on earth between birth and
death, and another kind of biography—a macrocosmic one—the
existence between death and rebirth, moving through the
planetary spheres as soon as the 'mortal coil' is discarded. The
individuality then lives in and through a kind of spiritual
geography. In an earthly biography the earthly conditions under
which a personality has incarnated have to be considered. In
England we speak of 'Constable country' or 'Thomas Hardy
country'. Or the poets from the Lake District, Wordsworth and
Coleridge in Grasmere, Ruskin at Coniston Water. We see certain
characteristics and the flavour of the landscape deeply ingrained
in these writers and their writing. Or we might compare the east
coast of England to Cornwall on the west coast. Further afield on
the Continent there is a vast difference between a man who treads
on limestone and chalk, as in the northern part of Austria, or one

* Rudolf Steiner, *The Last Address* (London, Rudolf Steiner Press, 1967)

whose foot meets with granite, as in the southern parts of Austria, right to the Dolomites, stretching further to the Swiss Alps.

These earthly conditions are as important to the true biography of man on earth as are the planetary conditions after death which form, transform and develop the individuality in the spirit-world.

If we follow Raphael's individuality through the planetary spheres with the help of Rudolf Steiner, we have the chance to look backwards and forwards. As from a watch-tower we observe this individuality from the past and into the future. We know that man passes through the Moon sphere and through the spheres of Mercury, Venus, the Sun, Mars, Jupiter, and Saturn. Together with the beings of these spheres, and together with other human souls who have departed from life on earth, Raphael elaborates his karma. He then turns back again to earthly existence. The eye of fantasy sees how he passes through the gate of death and how he enters the realm of the starry worlds, the realm of spiritual evolution, taking with him the power of his art—which on earth shone with the bright light of the stars.

We behold how Raphael enters the *Moon sphere*. We see how he comes into association with the spirits who live in the Moon sphere and who are the spiritual individualities of the great original leaders of Mankind (with whose wisdom Raphael, as Elijah, had been deeply inspired). He meets these Moon beings and he also meets all the souls with whom he had lived in earlier stages of earth evolution. We see how he unites himself spiritually with the spiritual origin of the earth. We see Raphael completely united with those whom he most loved in his Elijah existence, because it was they who set the goal for the life of the earth.

On his wandering through the *Mercury sphere* we find him in association with the great cosmic healers. He transforms for his spirituality the power to create what is infinitely whole and healthy in colour and line. Raphael *purified* mankind in the *light of the world*. Novalis *purged it of sin* in the *word of life*. Raphael did not depict the form of the cross in the crucifixion, but in the compositon of the *Sistine Madonna*. The cross is here the underlying formative principle, combined with other figures such as the triangle, pentagram and circle. He saw with his artist's eye the cosmic, not the earthly, cross. The physical body of Christ does not hang upon it in his paintings. He saw from the spirit the glorification in death, the triumph, the healing life-begetting form

of the divine Creator power. All that he had painted, whether on
canvas or as a fresco on the walls; all his work that was so radiant
with light showed itself now to him in the great connection with
the beings of the Mercury sphere.

Thus was he, who on earth had unfolded so great a love for art,
whose soul had been aflame with love for colour and for line, now
transported into the *sphere of Venus*, which in turn bore him
across to the *Sun*, to that Sun existence which lived in all his
incarnations so far as they are known to us. For it was from the Sun
that he, as prophet Elijah, brought to mankind through the
medium of his own people the truth of the Sun as the goal of all
existence.

Novalis expressed it in the words of life: 'Love is the goal of
world history, the Amen of the universe.'

All that Raphael has painted in shining light for the followers of
Christ pours its rays unto the cosmic transformation of the human
heart. He passes through the zenith of his life in spirit worlds. He
is able to live over again the central and most exalted part of his
destiny—the initiation through Christ into 'Lazarus-John.'[33]

What Raphael had carried so far as the foundation of his life
penetrates the *sphere of Jupiter*. In this sphere he is able with
wisdom to enter in understanding with the spirit who afterwards
became Goethe. As Novalis he said of him: 'In Goethe freedom
grows with culture. The poet is but the highest stage of the
thinker. The division between the poet and the thinker is only on
the surface; in reality there is a deep invisible union. For the truth
and the discipline within him are even more exemplary than they
seem.' Here in the Jupiter sphere Raphael's individuality, on its
transit to Novalis, is deeply imbued with Goethe's concept of
metamorphosis, his morphilogical thought about polarity and
enhancement to be finally led to *world being* and *world thought*
into the realm of 'Magical Idealism'. On the other hand Raphael's
use of colour inspired Goethe to a totally new experience of
colour, and in the wisdom-filled sphere of Jupiter his own ideas
on the theory of colour were born. He saw in colours—as
opposed to Newton—not the diffused, broken up particles of the
white ray of light, but the 'deeds and sufferings of the Elohim', the
Sun spirits; and that colour arises through the interpenetration of
light and darkness.

In the very centre of his 'last address' Rudolf Steiner placed 'the awakening of Lazarus'. Never before had Rudolf Steiner linked together the individualities of John the Baptist and Lazarus-John in the manner in which he did it in this last lecture. We are pointed to the fact that the great individuality Elijah/John the Baptist plays a tremendous part in this 'awakening of Lazarus-John'. Rudolf Steiner spoke of John the Baptist many times before, but never of the representing sequence in consecutive lives of the same individuality; Elijah—John the Baptist—Raphael—Novalis. This was the first series of reincarnations declared by Rudolf Steiner and never added to by other examples until the very last months of his life.[34] In their various ways these four historic personalities were the lives of the heraldic angel of the Christ.

Before I approach the dramatic raising of Lazarus I need a stepping stone, or a foundation stone, or a meaningful bridge-passage. We read in St John's Gospel, (when the Jews ask Jesus for a sign) 'he said unto them, Destroy this temple, and in three days I will raise it up. Then said the Jews forty and six years was this temple in building, and wilt thou rear it up in three days? But he spake of the temple of his body. When therefore he was risen from the dead, the disciples remembered that he had said this unto them.' (John 2:18-22).

In this apparent miracle of the raising of Lazarus is depicted a *new act of initiation* at the dawn of the new Christian era in which initiations were superseded altogether by *inner develop-ment*. Never before the 'last address' did Rudolf Steiner refer to another incarnation of Lazarus, nor did he ever connect him with the Baptist—although only once, as early as 1902, did Rudolf Steiner tentatively touch on a previous incarnation of Lazarus. Yet it is definitely indicated that Lazarus, the most intimate disciple of Christ, had matured sufficiently for the awakening of the Word in him.

The mystery which surrounds Lazarus became a challenge to me. Who was Lazarus? I went in search of him and found some help in the explanation of an essay by Dr Kirchner-Bockholt reprinted in the News Sheet of *Das Goetheanum* (1 December 1963). Of Lazarus, St John the Evangelist does not tell us much except that he followed Christ quietly. He was the rich youth whom Christ instructed to give away all his riches if he wanted to enter the Kingdom of God. Lazarus wanted to sacrifice his wealth to the Christ; not only his material, but also the wealth of his soul because he was longing for a renewal of everything that lived in him through Christ. He brought the great wealth of his soul from previous incarnations, and Kirchner-Bockholt chose one of the many incarnations which in particular presents his deep devotion and will to sacrifice. She chose one to which Rudolf Steiner himself pointed in an early lecture. In one of his previous incarnations Lazarus was the Phoenician master-builder Hiram. We know him well from Steffen's drama, *Hiram and Solomon**. Hiram and Solomon present the Cain and Abel stream. Solomon, the Abelite, still lives in a dream-like clairvoyance, which made it impossible for so long to erect a temple which, in all details should be representative of the evolution of mankind. For this building Solomon called for the master-builder Hiram of Tyros, who was a son of Cain. Hiram had developed so far in the practise of the arts that he was already mature for a knowledge of the spiritual world. And therefore he was called for the building of Solomon's temple. Although the outward form of the temple was perfect the cast of the Holy of Holies in the centre of the temple failed. Instead of a harmonization of the seven metals, so that they could serve the 'Word' again, a chaotic conflagration broke out into which Hiram leapt to save the cast. But in doing so he arrived at the centre of the earth, to Cain, his forefather, in whom he had found the archetype of the cosmic body. Cain took the golden triangle from his forehead and gave it to Hiram.

All this takes place in the deepest recesses of Lazarus' soul. He follows Hiram to his death in the Logos, and he hears the plea of Hiram that the logos should build up his body anew. Now we have returned to our building stone, or foundation stone: 'but he spoke of the temple of his body'.

Rudolf Steiner painted in a radiant picture how, after the death of John the Baptist, his spiritual being overshadowed the Spirit of the Disciples; but after the 'last address' he replied to a question from Dr Ludwig Noll (who together with Dr Ita Wegman, attended him during his illness). Dr Noll was given the following verbal explanation by Rudolf Steiner: 'At the Awakening of Lazarus, the spiritual being John the Baptist, who since his death had been over-shadowing the spirit of the disciples, penetrated

* Albert Steffen, *Hiram and Solomon* (Dornach, Verlag für Schöne Wissenschaften, 1970)

from above into Lazarus himself, as far as the consciousness soul; the being of Lazarus himself from below, intermingled with the spiritual being of John the Baptist from above. After the awakening of Lazarus, the Being is Lazarus-John, the Disciple whom the Lord loved.'

When the spirit of John the Baptist penetrated Lazarus he found in him the perfect human being of the future. For Lazarus had already advanced to the consciousness soul development, and the secret of the golden triangle of Cain's forehead became the three higher stages of man: his spirit-self, life-spirit and spirit-man.

When we look back into olden times, we see rising up before us within the traditions of Judaism the prophetic figure of Elijah. We know what enormous significance the prophet Elijah had for the people of the Old Testament and therewith for all mankind. We know how he set before them the goal of the destiny of their existence. And we have shown how the being of Elijah appeared again so that Christ Himself could give him the initiation for the evolution of mankind. For the being of Elijah appeared again as Lazarus-John (they are in truth one and the same figure). And we can see further that this being appears once more in that painter who let his artistic power unfold in marvellous depths of tenderness, in the deeply Christian impulse that lived in Raphael, impelling into colour and form the very nature and being of Christianity itself—and how this impulse rose again in the poet Novalis. In the poet Novalis stands revealed, in wondrously beautiful words, what Raphael had placed before mankind in colours and forms of rarest loveliness. His *Transfiguration*, Christ between Moses and Elijah upon the mountain, points to this. It was Raphael's last work. As he was dying he was still painting the countenance of Christ. This victory Raphael took with him in picture-form through the gate of death.

And now what remains is to look into the future, right into our own time. Novalis experienced both past and future within the present. What was wonder-filled wisdom for the Ancients was to transmute itself into love. Whoever thinks the laws of reincarnation through can see that the paintings Novalis created within himself had been carried over from out of an earlier life. If we think of Raphael and Novalis together we discover that the sphere of poetry approaches that of painting through imagination, and the sphere of painting that of poetry through inspiration.

Intuition, however, which recognises the individual within the earthly personalities of Raphael and Novalis, reveals the common source from which both draw: the Logos. If we contemplate the mission of Raphael we must see it together with his later poet-form as Novalis, whom Rudolf Steiner calls our helper. Raphael helps to exalt light to life as painter; Novalis helps to exalt the word to love as poet. It is inspiring and encouraging to think that men will arm themselves in the right way for the battle against evil by allowing the pictures and words of such an individuality to live on within. They strengthen us to become victorious over the dragon-kind that now grows rampant around us: the 'animal that rises out of the abyss'. The most sacred traditions refer to this when they say that Elijah will appear to take up the battle against the Antichrist.

Amongst Novalis' work we also find the *Last Judgement*. He created in advance through poetry what will one day become the experience of all mankind: the 'war of all against all' and the Rescuer who appears. This is found in Judaic, Christian and German tradition. Even in the texts of Russian songs can this prophecy be found. And always they allude to the mission which Elijah is to undertake. As folk-spirit of the ancient Hebrew people we hear that, three days before the coming of the Messiah as the Risen Christ, Elijah will climb the highest mountain in Judea and blow upon a great horn so that it is heard over the whole world. And the Judgement will then take place.

In the archaic chronicles of the German *Voluspa* Elijah opposes Halir, the Hell-dweller, as the way-preparer for the Christ, the super earthly saviour. In Christian tradition the Archangel Michael sounds the trumpet three times, and at the third trumpet call the dead quickly arise.

Through spiritual science the validity of such pictures is confirmed. They must be brought to the humanity of today and tomorrow in a new way. This Rudolf Steiner did in his 'last address' where he formed the tremendous link from Elijah to the Michael stream of our time.

Therefore I shall end with the tremendous vision of the future: the proclamation of Elijah-John, Raphael, Novalis. It is a call to

Europe as the centre; it is Novalis' vision of a new brotherhood in his work *Christianity or Europe.**

'Old and new worlds are joined in battle; the inadequacy and incompetence of our national organisations have become apparent in terrible phenomena. It is impossible that worldly powers should bring themselves into balance. A third element, that is worldly and super-earthly at the same time, can absolve this task. Between the battling forces no peace can be sealed, all peace is only an illusion, merely a laying down of arms (or raising them again in defence). From the standpoint of the cabinets or popular consciousness no unity is thinkable. Let neither power nor hope destroy the other. All conquests here are of no avail, but the innermost citadel of each empire lies not behind earthly walls and cannot be taken by force.

Who knows if we have had enough of war; but it will never cease if we do not grasp the palm branch which a spiritual power alone can hold out to us. More blood will flow over Europe until the nations recognise their frightful insanity which drives them vainly in circles, and celebrate with hot tears a festival of peace upon the smoking battle fields. Only true religion can awaken Europe once more, can reconcile the peoples and install Christianity with new splendour in its function of ministering peace.

When and how soon? That is not to be asked. Only patience! It will, it must come, the holy time of eternal peace, when the New Jerusalem shall be the capital of the world. And until then be serene and full of courage in the midst of the dangers of the times, brothers of my belief. Proclaim with word and deed Christ's divine Gospel, and to that eternal immeasurable faith remain true even unto death.'

* Novalis, *Hymns to the Night and other Selected Writings*, (New York, Bobbs-Merrill Company, 1960).

12
The Christian Substance in Rudolf Steiner's *Philosophy of Freedom*

'And being warned of God in a dream that they should not return to Herod, they departed into their own country another way' (St Matthew 2:12).

How often have we not heard and read these words without much further thought than that the Three Wise Men of the East wanted to avoid Herod and save the child Jesus. And yet, after they had given away all their ancient 'Star-wisdom'[35] (which had dimmed and become tradition, but still guided their way until the star disappeared at the stable where a child was born which was to bring a new beginning, a new *spiritual impulse* into the world), after they had realised that a God had become man, could the Three Kings ever have returned to their homeland in the *same* old way? Or is the indication in the Gospel a pointer that something entirely *new* appeared on earth with the incarnation of Christ Jesus? This was what these three representatives of ancient cultures were aware of and it changed their future life and destiny. They returned 'another' way as different individualities who had received the new Christ Impulse after they had given away all their ancient wisdom—represented as gold, frankincense and myrrh. The Three Kings died soon after their meeting with the Christ child. An ancient baptistry depicts this event. Engraved in relief one perceives the Three Kings in a boat crossing the waters. This is the indication of a baptism, a transformation into a new state of awareness, a 'change of the disposition of the soul' as John the Baptist admonished. This crossing meant either death or initiation. In the case of the Kings it meant both. As the Magi in pre-Christian times they were so organised that only one third of their being was on earth; two thirds however still dwelt in spirit worlds. The meeting with the *new* Christ Impulse changed all that.

The Three Kings were soon reborn, deeply imbued with the Christ Impulse and they were initiated in their new incarnations by Christ himself, who awakened their egos and they became the bearers of the esoteric Christ Impulse of the future.

From the inner being of the Kings and its transformation, we look out into the world of their time. This world is described as frosty, wintery, dark and bleak. But was this of necessity a natural condition of a wintery climate as we know it in midwinter, or is it not more likely the description of a spiritual climate as it were; a historical moment in time when all spiritual forces, which lighted and warmed past cultures, had withdrawn and Christ was born into the cold spiritual darkness as the Light which the darkness could not comprehend? We know that 'spiritual climate' as the receding horizon of spirit gold and warmth, '*Kali Yuga*' (the Dark Age whose dawn began in the year 3101 BC and ended in the year AD1899). In the *Michael Mystery** we read that this descent occurred in four stages; from the highest, that of being and revelation, the spirit has arrived in the 'world of creation'. With the withdrawal of spirit light, warmth and life, the earth was plunged into darkness and the icy grip of *death*.

Today we must realise that without darkness and the forces of death man would never have gained *consciousness*. It is precisely the absence of light which makes man conscious of the light.

How can we trace historically, in a developing grade of consciousness, the gradual spiritual decline in the world and in man? Rudolf Steiner describes this act in his lecture given at Arnhem, 19 July 1924.† 'In ancient Greece an order was issued to Plato to confine mystery wisdom to human thoughts. This Plato could not do. He could communicate the mysteries to man in a wonderful, radiant, imaginative language, in spirit-images, but he could not develop the logic of thought.'

Plato had grown old and realised that his exalted teaching, the extract of mystery teaching, came to men who were already differently organised and could not receive this wisdom in ideas formed as imaginations. Therefore he had to give over this ancient form of knowledge to his pupil Aristotle. In him Plato saw the man

* Rudolf Steiner, *The Michael Mystery* (New York, St George Publications, 1984)
† Rudolf Steiner, *Karmic Relationships Volume VI* (London, Rudolf Steiner Press, 1971)

of the future who governed the new kind of language necessary
for the organisation of men of the future, that of the intellect.

It was Aristotle's task to prepare the descent of the cosmic
intelligence into human intelligence at the order of Michael in the
last pre-Christian age. Through Aristotelianism the earthly intelligence was scaled off the cosmic intelligence. (In the original
German Rudolf Steiner uses the word *heraus-Schalen* which is the
verb of *Schale*. Today we speak of *Gehirn-Schale*, the cranium or
skull.) What later on was called the 'logic of Aristotle' was the
extricating of the thought skeleton which became human
intelligence, on which the thinking of all subsequent centuries
was based.

'And now we must conceive that through this single deed the
Michael Impulse culminated: the earthly human intelligence was
established and was imprinted upon those people who at that
time were ready to receive the cosmopolitan impulse.'*

It is important to remark here that it was Rudolf Steiner's
lifelong concern to show that a rift between Plato and Aristotle
never took place. He points out that what history sees as a rift
between these great men never existed. On the contrary: it is of
utmost importance that, as in the past and even more so in the
future, Platonism and Aristotelianism should work together;
whether on earth or in the spiritual world, or with one soul
incarnated on earth and the other living after death in the spiritual
world. In all meetings of the Michael School,[36] especially from the
fifteenth to the eighteenth century, these two streams were
always there together and will have to work together in future,
especially after the end of the twentieth century.

In the middle of Kali Yuga, the Dark Age, the Mystery of
Golgotha took place. From then on man began for the first time to
feel the significance of death—that earthly life has indeed an
ending. This was at the beginning only a perceptive experience
and was not formulated in philosophical or scientific terms. But
through the death-experience, reason and intellect became an
essential part of human evolution. Intellect is dependent upon the
fact that the human being can die. The absorption of death into
life—that is the secret of Golgotha. Man learnt death as a
constituent of life; as an experience which gives strength to life.

* Rudolf Steiner, *Karmic Relationships Volume VI* (London, Rudolf Steiner Press, 1971)

We in modern times have the faculty of intellect, but in the operations of the intellect we are not alive in a real sense. When man is thinking he does not truly live; he pours his life into empty intellectual forms. He needs a strong robust sense of life in the region where *moral impulses* spring up.

When all spiritual activities seemed doomed to die at the end of Kali Yuga a *new light* began to shine and radiate with warmth. At that point in time Rudolf Steiner gave to the world his *Philosophy of Freedom.** This book is written out of the fully developed consciousness soul which can live in the etheric world. In it arise for the first time living thoughts which are so mighty that they can exist in spiritual worlds. They originate in *freedom*. In the act of thinking in freedom man does not pour out his life into empty intellectual forms which Rudolf Steiner calls the 'strongly marked shadow of its real nature'. In reality thinking is warm and luminous and penetrates deeply into the phenomena of the world. This penetration is brought about through the activity of thinking itself— *the power of love in its spiritual form.*

Moral impulses spring from the force of pure thinking, and here in the operations of pure thinking we understand the *reality* of freedom. *The Philosophy of Freedom* is essentially a moral philosophy indicating how pure thoughts in their highest form are essentially 'moral intuitions'. Dead thoughts filled with life may be led to their resurrection as moral impulses. If we turn towards thinking we find in it both *love* (feeling) and *freedom* (will) in the depth of its reality. To this extent such a philosophy is essentially *Christian*.

To attempt pure thinking man had to first of all become an independent thinker and develop autonomous thinking (*selbstandiges denken*) which is independent of our physical organisation and the disposition of our character, and is not determined by outer circumstances. Rudolf Steiner therefore calls it *pure* thinking. He points out that this thinking is able to observe freedom in a threefold way. In the *will* freedom is practised. In *feeling* freedom is experienced. In *thinking* freedom is known.

How does this act of knowledge take place today? We are organised in such a way that we *perceive* the outer world, which

* Rudolf Steiner, *The Philosophy of Freedom* (London, Rudolf Steiner Press, 1988)

confronts us as 'given', without engaging our activity; but we only
know by adding the spiritual entity through the creative activity
of the 'I'. In this union thinking is above subject and object. Rudolf
Steiner says of this thinking, which is an inner activity, that we
have in it 'the true spiritual communion, the union with the true
reality'.* Goethe called this act 'truth'.

If we go a step further in our observations we discover a further
aspect on the path of knowledge. What happens if this true
communion of the 'I' and the world takes place? In this activity,
when 'world-knowledge' becomes 'self-knowledge' and vice
versa, a *transubstantiation* of both takes place. In every act of
cognition the perceptible object of the world is transmuted
(modified) into our spiritual nature. This is the whole reality. A
perceptive picture which has been thoroughly permeated by the
experience of thinking leads us into *reality*.

Very rightly Karl Unger says in his *Language of the Consciousness Soul*†: *Jede Erkenntnis verwandelt den Erkennenden und
auch das Erkannte*: 'Every act of cognition transforms both the
individual engaged in it and whatever its object.' The establishing
of true reality is a *spiritual communion*. Every true act of
cognition is *transubstantiation*.

In a lecture on freedom and love, Rudolf Steiner goes so far as
to say of thinking and willing: 'When thinking has become *pure* it
can also be designated as *pure will*. Nevertheless we have to
differentiate in the actual interpretation: freedom plus will
radiating into thinking. Love equals thought permeating the will
(devotion to the outer world)'. If we raise ourselves in pure
thinking to the will then we have become inwardly free. Thinking
does not receive its content from outside. It has become pure
will; it sets its own content and its own goal. It has become '*moral
intuition*'. Inasmuch as we strengthen the will in thinking we
prepare ourselves for '*moral imagination*'. In it pure thought
permeates the will and this becomes the source of a free deed
through 'moral technique'. Everything which man can fulfil from
the spiritual world is grounded in moral intuition, and through it

* Rudolf Steiner, *The Boundaries of Natural Science* (New York, Anthroposophic
Press, 1983)
†·Karl Unger, *Language of the Consciousness Soul* (New York, St George Publica-
tions, 1983)

man is in reality filled with the spiritual world. 'Through a free deed something appears on earth which is not of the earth.'

'If the soul in our time has the right place in earth evolution it has to develop on the one hand a strong impulse to freedom and on the other hand a strong impulse to an inner experience of the Mystery of Golgotha. These two things belong together.'*

And at Norrkoepping, Sweden, he said: '*The Philosophy of Freedom* can be considered as the ripest fruit of the Tree of Knowledge. The Fall of Man is the first religious gift which mankind has received. The second is the Mystery of Golgotha.'

A remark of Leonardo da Vinci's here comes to mind which unites both: 'The great love is born out of great knowledge of a thing one loves; and if you do not know it, you cannot love it or only sparsely love it.'

To bring this study on *The Philosophy of Freedom* to a close we have to remember also what Rudolf Steiner calls 'Pauline thought' in the domain of the theory of knowledge. As St Paul was born on 6 January, the Three Kings day, we end as we began, although from a different aspect. At the end of the lecture cycle *The Karma of Materialism*† we read as Pauline thought:

> 'Man having entered the world through the first Adam, has the world before him in an inferior form and will first experience it in its true form through what he can become through Christ, the second Adam. This is Pauline knowledge carried over into the domain of philosophy. Pauline philosophy does not set up a theological formula, but what really matters is the *mode of thinking*. I am justified in saying that the Pauline Spirit lives in the books *Truth and Science* and *The Philosophy of Freedom* although they are entirely philosophical in character. From this philosophy it is possible to find the bridge leading to the *Christ-Spirit*, just as from natural science the bridge leading to the *Father-Spirit* can be found. But the change must come from within.'

* Rudolf Steiner, *The Human Soul in Relation to World Evolution* (New York, Anthroposophic Press, 1984).

† Rudolf Steiner, *The Karma of Materialism* (New York, London, Anthroposophic Press, Rudolf Steiner Press, 1985)

It was once in pre-Christian times the task of Aristotle to confine the 'golden writ' of Mystery Wisdom into the cavity of the skull for the immediate future of the evolution of mankind.

After the Mystery of Golgotha it was the self-appointed task of the same individuality to free thinking of its earthly fetters and make it into a spirit-filled activity,[37] as the Christ bearer in freedom and in love, to carry it as a flaming torch into the future of earth evolution.

Editor's Notes

1. The spiritual record of all events, thoughts and actions, often referred to by Rudolf Steiner and other spiritual teachers. It should be noted that the records do not exist on the physical plane, and that a high degree of occult training is required for a clear, direct perception of their contents.

2. Steiner explains the apparently conflicting accounts of the child-hood of Jesus in the Matthew and Luke Gospels by the revelation that there existed two separate Jesus children. The two united and became one with the death of the child in the Matthew Gospel. The profound meaning of this is developed at some length in Steiner's lectures on Christology. See, for example: Rudolf Steiner, *From Jesus to Christ* (London, Rudolf Steiner Press, 1973).

3. According to Steiner, the fear that Attila the Hun's invasion of Europe caused the local population, later manifested itself as the physical illness of leprosy. The Hun armies also brought strong will-forces with them. The demonic nature of these forces had to be cleansed by the development of moral forces and the development of Christianity.

4. See: George Adams, *The Mysteries of the Rose Cross* (London, Temple Lodge Press, 1989).

5. Many divergent writings exist on Christian Rosenkreutz and the Rosicrucian Movement. Steiner described the role of the true Rosicrucians as cultivating 'an understanding of the Christ Mystery in a way suited to the new era', in the tradition of the Order of the Grail and the Order of the Templars.

6. The Therapeutae and the Essenes were both religious orders existing at the time of Christ's incarnation on earth. The Therapeu-tae were known particularly as healers, while it is believed that the Essenes were the authors of the *Dead Sea Scrolls*. Steiner tells us that John the Baptist was an Essene, and that Jesus of Nazareth was schooled by the order as a youth.

7. Steiner clearly rejects the notion of a physical second coming of

Christ. Rather, the Christ will appear in the etheric sphere; see Rudolf Steiner, *The Reappearance of Christ in the Etheric* (New York, Anthroposophic Press, 1983).

8. A specialist on the history of Western Asia.

9. According to Steiner, the flood of Atlantis actually took place and, as Lona Truding remarks, is to be found in the Bible in the story of Noah's ark.

10. Steiner is often misrepresented over his views on race. The most pertinent point he makes for our time is that, with the development of individual consciousness, the significance of race gradually diminishes.

11. The etherisation of the blood allows ultimately for a transformation of thinking. For an expansion of this theme see: Rudolf Steiner, *The Etherisation of the Blood* (London, Rudolf Steiner Press, 1985).

12. The official journal of the international Anthroposopical Society, published in German in Dornach, Switzerland.

13. The authority of the original kings, or rather 'priest-kings', was based on their role as communicators with the divine world. Hence the 'divine right' of kings to rule.

14. See note 2. The Solomon Jesus referred to in the text is the child from the Matthew Gospel, the reincarnation of the Zarathustra individuality. See: Rudolf Steiner, *The Gospel of St Matthew* (London, New York, Rudolf Steiner Press, Anthroposophic Press, 1985).

15. The Foundation Stone Meditation was given by Rudolf Steiner during the laying of the foundation stone for the building of the second Goetheanum, after the first building had been burnt down. The meditation is reproduced in: Rudolf Steiner, *The Foundation Stone Meditation* (London, Rudolf Steiner Press, 1979).

16. The Western concept of reincarnation differs from the Eastern in that it introduces the idea of freedom which creates the possibility of overcoming one's karma and moving on. Steiner also acknowledges the being of Christ as the 'Lord of Karma' (see: Rudolf Steiner, *From Jesus to Christ* (op. cit.)

17. The Christmas Foundation meeting in 1923 constituted the establishment of the Anthroposophical Society as an international organisation with its headquarters at the Goetheanum in Dornach, Switzerland.

18. See particularly the various lecture cycles on the Gospels.

19. Steiner tells us that man was once an instinctive creature, strongly tied to the spiritual worlds by a natural clairvoyance. The 'Fall', and subsequent banishment from the Garden of Eden described in Genesis is a picture of the gradual evolution towards self-consciousness and the freedom of the individual.

20. The terms 'ancient Sun' and 'ancient Moon' refer to vast epochs of time (not to the present physical planetary bodies). For a full description of these ancient periods of time and their significance see: Rudolf Steiner, *Occult Science, An Outline* (London, Rudolf Steiner Press, 1984).

21. See previous chapter, 'A Miracle for Our Time'.

22. The 'Ego' referred to here is not to be confused with the present-day popular usage of the term, but is rather a translation of the German *ich*, 'I'. This is the higher self, capable of responsibility and present in all human beings. For a full explanation of the various members of man's being see: Rudolf Steiner, *Occult Science, An Outline* (op. cit.)

23. The mystery of the 'I Am' is explained more fully in: Rudolf Steiner, *The Gospel of St John* (New York, Anthroposophic Press, 1973).

24. This is not a direct biblical quotation.

25. All substantial biblical quotations are taken from the Authorised King James Version.

26. The author is referring to an ancient rite, not to be confused with Anthroposophy, and certainly not recommended by Steiner for modern day purposes!

27. This is not a direct biblical quotation.

28. At this point in the text the author refers to two titles on Joan of Arc: Andre Guevin, *The Mysteries of Joan of Arc* (London, Heinemann, 1961) and Pierre de Sermoise, *Joan of Arc and her Secret Missions* (London, Robert Hale, 1973).

29. For further information on St Francis and morality see: Rudolf Steiner, *The Spiritual Foundation of Morality* (N. Vancouver, Steiner Book Centre, 1986).

30. See the chapter 'The Mysteries of the Black Sea'.

31. Human souls pass through the planetary spheres after death. See: Rudolf Steiner, *Between Death and Rebirth* (New York, Anthroposophic Press, 1985).

32. In his last address, Steiner describes the series of incarnations of a particular individuality (see footnote for reference). This spiritual being incarnated as Elijah, John the Baptist, Raphael and Novalis.

33. The term 'Lazarus-John' is used by Rudolf Steiner. He tells us that the Lazarus who 'rose from the dead' in the Gospel of St John (or rather went through an ancient form of initiation) is the writer of that Gospel.

34. In the deeply esoteric 'karma' lectures, Steiner describes the incarnations and karma of various well-known individualities such as Karl Marx and Voltaire. See: Rudolf Steiner, *Karmic Relationships, Volumes I to VIII* (London, Rudolf Steiner Press).

35. The knowledge of the meaning of the movement of the planets and the zodiac. Today a diluted form of this is found in the science of astrology.
36. The 'school' is in the divine sphere, under the rule of the Archangel Michael—the Time Spirit of the present age.
37. The author is alluding to the popular conception in anthroposophical circles that Steiner himself was the reincarnation of Aristotle and St Thomas Aquinas. It should be noted that Steiner never publicly confirmed this theory.